THE GAME OF CHESS

Harry Golombek was born in London in 1911, and educated at Wilson's Grammar School and London University. He became boy chess champion of London in 1929, and two years later was the youngest player ever to win the Surrey Championship. He is one of Britain's leading players, and figured fourteen times in the prize list of the British Championship, from equal second in 1938 to first in 1955. He was British Champion in 1947, 1949, and 1955. He is also one of Britain's foremost international masters, and was captain and first of the British team at the Helsinki International Team Tournament 1952, captain at Amsterdam in 1954, first board in Moscow in 1956, and captain again at Munich 1958, Leipzig 1960, and Golden Sands 1962. He has written books on many aspects of the game, and is recognized as Britain's leading theorist. An authority on rules, he was appointed by the International Chess Federation to act as judge at the World Championship matches in Moscow 1954, 1957, 1958, 1960, 1961, and 1963. He has translated *The Art of the Middle Game* by Keres and Kotov, which is available in Penguins. He is Chess Correspondent of *The Times* and the *Observer* and he was awarded the OBE in 1966 for services to chess.

D1390651

H. GOLOMBEK

THE GAME OF CHESS

PENGUIN BOOKS

Penguin Books Ltd, Harmondsworth, Middlesex, England
Penguin Books, 625 Madison Avenue, New York, New York 10022, U.S.A.
Penguin Books Australia Ltd, Ringwood, Victoria, Australia
Penguin Books Canada Ltd, 2801 John Street, Markham, Ontario L3R 1B4, Canada
Penguin Books (N.Z.) Ltd, 182–190 Wairau Road, Auckland 10, New Zealand

—

First published 1954
Reprinted 1955, 1957, 1959, 1961
Second edition 1963
Reprinted 1965, 1966, 1969, 1970, 1972, 1973 (twice), 1974, 1976, 1977

—

Copyright © H. Golombek, 1954, 1963

—

Made and printed in Great Britain
by Cox & Wyman Ltd,
London, Reading and Fakenham
Set in Monotype Times

CONTENTS

CHAPTER 1

INTRODUCTION TO THE GAME

CHESS, 'the game which', says Voltaire, 'reflects most honour on human wit', arose in the fifth century A.D. in north-west India. No more precise indication can be given as to its origin and it is not known what bright spirit invented the idea of the game. It was then called 'chaturanga' and though the game differed in some respects from the modern version it was clearly chess. No evidence exists for its having been played earlier and the occasional rumour that crops up to the effect that it was played in old Egyptian times has no foundation in fact.

In the sixth century it spread from India to Persia and a little later in the same century the Arabs learnt the game. Chess entered Europe round about the tenth century by three main ways: (1) to Italy across the trade routes of the Mediterranean; (2) to Spain from North Africa; (3) from Turkey through the Balkans. The first two paths joined up in France and from there the game spread to Germany and England. Chess came to England with the Norman Conquest and the first reference to it in English literature is found, somewhat late, in 1150 in a poem *De Shaki ludo*. The game appears to have become popular here in late medieval times, and indeed one of the first books printed in English on any subject was a chess book – Caxton's *The Game and Playe of the Chesse*, published in 1474.

By the seventeenth century the game had settled exactly into its modern form, from which it is unlikely to depart. In practice the variations within the given laws are inexhaustible, so that there is neither reason nor temptation to alter it.

HOW TO PLAY

The game of chess is played on a square board itself composed of 64 squares coloured alternately black and white. Each player moves a piece once and then allows his opponent to move – i.e. they move alternately. The two players each have 16 men at their disposal so that at the beginning of the game there are 32 pieces in all on the board.

POSITION AT THE START OF THE GAME

These 32 pieces are originally placed as in the diagram (Diagram 1).

INITIAL POSITIONS

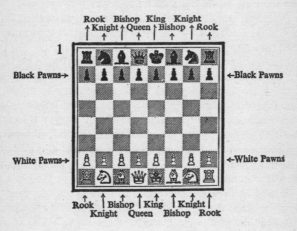

Note that the board is always set so that the extreme right-hand square to the player is White.

Each player has 8 Pawns which are on the second rank. These Pawns are the lowest in value of all the pieces and those of higher value appear on the first, or back, rank as follows:

In each corner is a Rook, sometimes called a Castle, shown in the diagram by the symbol ♖ ♜.

Next to each Rook is a Knight with the symbol ♘ ♞.

Next to each Knight is a Bishop with the symbol ♗ ♝.

Fourth from the left (from White's point of view) or fourth
from the right (viewing it from Black's side) is the Queen
with the symbol ♕ ♛. Note that this piece should always
be initially placed on a square of its own colour.

Fourth from the right (from White's point of view) or fourth
from the left (from Black's point of view) is the King with
the symbol ♔ ♚. This should always be placed initially
on a square of the opposite colour.

OBJECT OF THE GAME

Each player can capture his opponent's pieces with his own and
the object of the game is to place the opponent's King in such a
position that it cannot avoid being captured. This is known as
checkmate. A piece effects a capture by occupying the square
on which an enemy piece is placed.

HOW THEY MOVE

The King

This moves one square at a time in any direction as in the
diagram (Diagram 2). It cannot move into a position where it

2

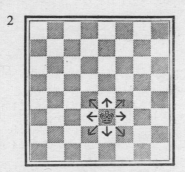

The King's move

may be captured and a piece that threatens to capture the King is said to be giving it 'check'. Hence two Kings can never be on adjacent squares. Hence, too, the King is at once the most vulnerable and the most valuable piece on the board. (For another specialized move of the King see under *Castling* on page 12.)

The Queen

Moves horizontally or vertically or along the diagonals for any number of squares as in the diagram (Diagram 3) and since

3   4

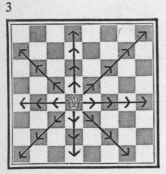   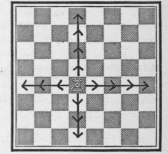

The Queen's move   The Rook's move

it commands the greatest number of squares (a maximum of 27) it is the most powerful piece on the board.

The Rook

Moves horizontally or vertically any number of squares as in the diagram (Diagram 4) and since it controls the next greatest number of squares to the Queen (a maximum of 14) it is the next most powerful piece. (For another specialized move of the Rook see under *Castling* on page 12.)

The Bishop

Moves any number of moves along the diagonals as in the

10

diagram (Diagram 5). It therefore follows that it can never change from the colour of the square on which it is initially placed.

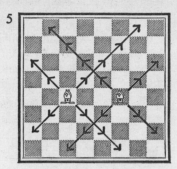

The Bishop's move

The Knight

This piece has a composite move. It moves two squares, horizontally or vertically, and then another square, vertically or horizontally, as in the diagram (Diagram 6).

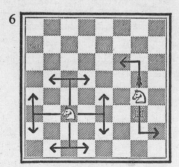

The Knight's move

It has the property peculiar to itself of being able to jump over any other piece.

11

Castling

This special type of move was introduced in the sixteenth century in order to make the game more dynamic and lively. It is a joint move of the King and Rook during which they pass over each other. In the case of King-side castling, the King is moved two squares to the right and the Rook (from the King side) two squares to the left. In Queen-side castling, the King is moved two squares to the left and the Rook (from the Queen side) three squares to the right. (See Diagrams 7, 7a, 7b.)

CASTLING

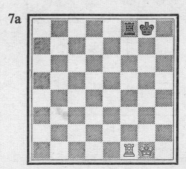

Position after King-side castling

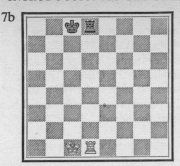

Position after Queen-side castling

Castling is impossible if (*a*) the King or Rook has already been moved, or (*b*) the King has to cross a square attacked by an enemy piece, or (*c*) the King is attacked by an enemy piece (i.e. is in check), or (*d*) the square on which the King eventually lands is attacked by an enemy piece, or (*e*) if there is another piece in the path of this manoeuvre.

The Pawn

The Pawn moves one square at a time except from its initial position when it can move either two squares at a time or one square. (See Diagram 8.) It must advance vertically and then

The Pawn's move

never move back, unlike all other pieces. Unlike all other pieces too it can only capture by a different type of move from its normal method of progress – that is, diagonally.

When it reaches the 8th rank it must be exchanged for another piece of its own colour, either a Queen, Rook, Bishop, or Knight, but not a King; hence, though it has the weakest form of movement, yet it has the fortunate compensation of being potentially the strongest piece on the board.

THE *EN PASSANT* RULE

The rule that a Pawn could move two squares initially was introduced in the sixteenth century – again so as to speed up events. We have seen that a Pawn captures diagonally and a relic of the old game remains in the *En Passant* rule. Should an enemy Pawn be on its fifth rank when one advances a Pawn two squares then this enemy Pawn can, if the opponent so desires, take off one's Pawn just as if it had moved only one square. This privilege can be exercised only at the very moment when the pawn is advanced two squares and cannot be deferred to a later stage in the game. (See Diagram 9.)

9

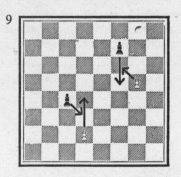

VALUE OF THE PIECES

Since the value of the pieces is based on the number of squares each commands one can make an estimate of their value in accordance with how far they can strike. The weakest on this count is the Pawn which can be classed as a single unit of power.

A Bishop and a Knight have about the same value and are worth three Pawns. But a Bishop is worth more than a Knight in positions that are not cluttered up by pieces (open positions) and a Knight is worth more than a Bishop in blocked or closed positions. As the game progresses and more and more exchanges are made, so the value of the Bishop increases. Hence potentially it is worth more than a Knight. If you look at the board a moment (Diagram 10) you will see that two Bishops in conjunction

10

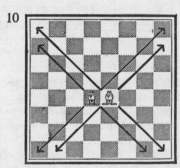

The Two Bishops

command a great deal of space and they therefore constitute a much valued possession.

A Rook is worth about five Pawns or slightly less than a Bishop plus a Knight. Two Rooks are worth rather more than a Queen.

A Queen is worth about nine Pawns and is therefore an extremely valuable piece. A fair exchange would be a Queen for Rook, Bishop, and a Pawn. However, a Queen is worth rather less than two Bishops and a Knight (or two Knights and a Bishop).

In view of their predominance Queens and Rooks are known as 'major pieces' and Knights and Bishops called 'minor pieces'.

The above gives one the following scale of values:

> Pawn   1
> Knight   3
> Bishop   3
> Rook   5
> Queen   9

Note that all these values are flexible and can change according to circumstances. So these are given only as a rough guide and the reader should not be too dogmatic in their use. It will be noticed that I have not given any value to the King, and the reason is quite simple – it is invaluable. You can at a pinch do without any of the pieces except the King, which you must guard with all your might and main.

NOTATION

Chess is more fortunate than most games in that a system of notation has been in existence for many years by which each game can be recorded. Consequently every important game, every game in international tournaments for example, has been preserved for us to play over.

The system used in Great Britain and the United States of America is known as the descriptive notation. A couple of definitions are necessary before this simple system can be explained. A rank is a series of eight squares running horizontally along the board. A file is a series of eight squares running vertically from top to bottom of the board.

Each square has a number from 1 to 8 according to where it is placed on the file; so that the first rank is entirely composed of squares numbered 1, the second rank of squares numbered 2, and so on. The files are differentiated from each other by the initial letter of the piece which was originally placed on square 1.

So looking at it from White's point of view the board is numbered as in Diagram 11. On the other hand, if you have the Black pieces then the board is numbered as in Diagram 12.

Black

11

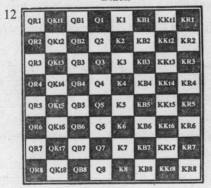

White

Black

12

White

Note that the *letters* for each square are the same for White and Black, but that the numbers are reversed.

With the squares of the board thus numbered all one has to do to indicate a move is to state which piece moves to which square. Pieces are indicated by their initial letter (in the case of

17

the Knight by the first and last letters to distinguish it from the King). A stroke – shows the actual moving process and a cross × indicates a capture. The process of castling is shown by 'Castles' or, more often, for the sake of brevity, O–O = Castles King side, and O–O–O = Castles Queen side. Two other abbreviations are ch for check, and *e.p.* for *en passant*.

So a game might start as follows:

1. P–K4

This means that White's first move was Pawn from K2 to the square K4.

1. ....　　　　　　　　　　P–K4

Black's Pawn from K2 goes to the square K4.

2. Kt–KB3

The Knight from White's KKt1 goes to the square KB3.

2. ....　　　　　　　　　　Kt–QB3

The Knight from Black's QKt1 goes to the square QB3.

3. B–Kt5

The Bishop from White's KB1 goes to the square QKt5. Note that it is not necessary to give the full name of this square as the Bishop can go only to this one of the Kt5s.

3. ....　　　　　　　　　　P–QR3

The Pawn from Black's QR2 goes to the square QR3.

4. B×Kt

The Bishop takes the Knight.

4. ....　　　　　　　　　　QP×B

The Pawn on Q2 takes the Bishop. Note that since another Pawn (that on QKt2) can capture the Bishop it is necessary to state which; had it been the other Pawn we would have said KtP×B.

5. O–O

The White King castles with the White Rook. This could also be indicated by 'Castles'.

    5. ....   B—Q3

The Black Bishop from KB1 goes to the square Q3.

    6. Kt—B3

The Knight from QKt1 goes to the square QB3. It is not necessary to say QKt—B3, since this is the only Knight that can go to B3.

    6. ....   Kt—K2

The Knight from KKt1 goes to the square K2.

    7. P—Q3

The Pawn from Q2 goes to the square Q3.

    7. ....   O—O

The Black King castles with the Black Rook.
We now have the following position (Diagram 13).

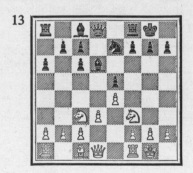

13

CHAPTER 2

THE SIMPLER ENDINGS

HOW TO CHECKMATE

THE ultimate object of the game is to deliver checkmate to the opposing King and for this it is usually necessary to have a superiority in forces.

The method of mating is always based on the principle of limiting the number of possible moves for the opponent's King.

Two Rooks

This is the simplest of all mates. Taking it from Diagram 14,

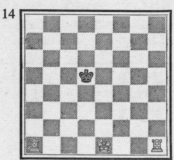

one plays:

> *1.* R — KR4

The first step in the limiting process; now the Black King is confined to four ranks.

> *1.* ....   K — K4
> *2.* R — QR5 ch

Depriving the King of another rank. Note that you use your pieces in *cooperation* with each other. This is the basis for success in the whole game.

2.	K – B3
3. R – KR6 ch	

Not R – QR6 ch, which would allow the King to escape back to the fourth rank.

3.	K – Kt2

Now he threatens to capture a Rook, so we must use a move to remove the Rook from the King's grasp.

4. R – Kt6*	K – B2
5. R – R7 ch	K – K1
6. R – Kt8 checkmate or, as it is frequently abbreviated, 'mate'.	

The Queen

The Queen being a very powerful piece it is very easy to administer mate with its aid; but, since it is only one unit and therefore covers only one field of action, it must be helped in its task by the King. This leads us to a fundamental rule in the end game: *Always use the King as much as possible.*

The way to mate here again depends on confining the opposing King to as few squares as possible. Starting with the position in Diagram 15, you should play:

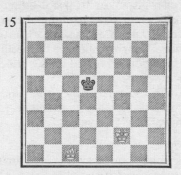

15

*Note this is QKt6; if the Rook went to KKt6 the notation would be R—Kt6 ch.

1. Q—B4

Limiting the King to the back four ranks.

1. ....   K—B4

If *1.* .... K—K3; *2.* Q—Kt5, and now the King has only three ranks to play in. Or *1.* .... K—B3; *2.* Q—K5, leaving the King still less space. However, after *1.* .... K—B4 it is best to make use of your own King to drive the other back, so

2. K—K3   K—Q4
3. K—Q3   K—K3
4. K—Q4

Depriving the Black King of the Q4 square and driving it back on to the second rank.

4. ....   K—K2
5. K—Q5   K—Q2
6. Q—B7 ch

We have done as much as we can with the White King for the moment and must now use the Queen to force the King back to the last rank.

6. ....   K—B1
7. K—B6   K—Kt1
8. Q—QKt7 mate.

One danger that must be avoided in giving mate with the Queen (or indeed with any other piece or pieces) is that of arriving at a position where the opposing solitary King cannot move at all. This is known as 'stalemate', in which case the game is only a draw. Suppose you have the position in Diagram 16. Now if you incautiously proceed on the principle of limiting your opponent's moves by

1. K—Kt6?*

you find that the Black King has no move, i.e. is stalemate and the game is a draw. Correct would be:

1. Q—Q7   K—Kt1
2. K—Kt6   K—R1
3. Q—B8 mate.

* A query is used to indicate a bad move and an exclamation mark for a good move.

22

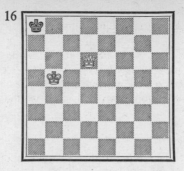

The Queen is such a powerful piece that it can give stalemate by itself. Thus, if in Diagram 17 you decide to limit your

opponent's moves by the dashing Q — B7 you again find you have overreached yourself and allowed a stalemate. Correct would be Q — R7 followed by the approach of your own King towards the other.

The Rook

This mate, since the Rook is a less powerful piece than the Queen, needs more help from the King. See Diagram 18.

1. K – B2

The King must be brought near to its enemy.

1.	K – Q5
2. K – B3	K – Q4

If *2.* .... K – Q6; *3.* R – Q1 ch, drives the King to the QB file, thereby cutting it off from the five files on the right of the board.

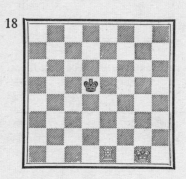

18

3. R – K4

Cutting the Black King off from White's half of the board.

3.	K – Q3
4. K – B4	

4. R – Q4 ch would be a useless check as Black's King would get back to the centre of the board and the first object to be attained in mating with the Rook is *to drive the King to a back rank or a file on the edge of the board.*

4.	K – Q4

If *4.* .... K – Q2; *5.* R – K5.

5. K – B5

Note the use of this quiet-looking move – a waiting move that forces back the Black King. The idea will recur again and again in many types of endings and is especially important in this.

24

5.	K – Q3

Or *5.* .... K – B4; *6.* K – K5.

6. R – K5	

The limiting process continues.

6.	K – B3

Had he played *6.* .... K – Q2 we would have further confined him by *7.* R – K6

7. K – K6	

The same idea as in White's 5th move.

7.	K – B2
8. R – B5 ch	K – Kt3

If *8.* .... K – Q1; *9.* R – B4, K – K1; *10.* R – B8 mate.

9. K – Q6	K – Kt2
10. R – B6	K – Kt1

Or *10.* .... K – R2; *11.* K – B7, K – R1; *12.* R – R6 mate.

11. R – B7	K – R1
12. K – B6	K – Kt1
13. K – Kt6	K – R1
14. R – B8 mate.	

Two Bishops

Here again the King must be driven to the edge of the board, but since the action of the Bishops is along the diagonals only *the King must be confined to a corner.*

The mating player must use his King as much as possible and in the worst configuration of pieces he can deliver mate in 18 moves. The classic example is that given by Berger as long ago as 1890. See Diagram 19.

1. B – Q1	

Bishops work best at a distance.

1.	K – K6
2. K – Kt2	K – Q7
3. B – QB2	

25

This and the following move cut the King off from the left half of the board.

3.	K — K6
4. K — B3	K — B6

Or *4.* .... K — K7; *5.* B — Kt5, K — B6; *6.* K — Q2, K — Kt5; *7.* B — K3, K — B6; *8.* B — KB5, K — Kt7; *9.* K — K2, K — Kt6; *10.* B — Kt5, K — Kt7; *11.* B — B4, K — Kt8; *12.* K — B3, K — B8; *13.* B — Q2, K — Kt8; *14.* K — Kt3, K — B8; *15.* B — Q3 ch, K — Kt8; *16.* B — K3 ch, K — R8; *17.* B — K4 mate.

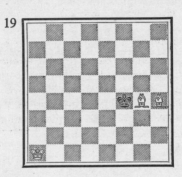

19

5. K — Q4	K — Kt5
6. B — K1	K — B6
7. B — Q3	K — B5
8. B — K4	K — Kt4
9. K — K5	K — Kt5
10. B — KB2	K — Kt4

If *10.* .... K — R6; *11.* K — B4, K — R7; *12.* K — B3, K — R6; (*12.* .... K — R8; *13.* K — Kt3 dis ch mate) *13.* B — Q3, K — R7; *14.* B — B1, K — R8; *15.* B — K3 (not *15.* K — Kt3, stalemate) *15.* .... K — R7; *16.* K — B2, K — R8; *17.* B — Kt2 ch, K — R7; *18.* B — B4 mate.

11. B — KB5	K — R3
12. K — B6	K — R4

Now a waiting move is necessary to get the Black King back to R3.

13. B—K6	K—R3
14. B—Kt4	K—R2
15. K—B7	

Note that this is the essential position for the King in the two Bishops mate. It must be a Kt's move away from the R square.

15.	K—R3
16. B—K3 ch	K—R2
17. B—B5 ch	K—R1
18. B—Q4 mate.	

The rules of chess state that you must administer mate in 50 moves in positions where such a mate can be forced within this number of moves. Otherwise, provided a Pawn has not been moved or a capture made during this period, a draw can be claimed. Here is a list of the forces with which one can normally force a mate against a solitary King.

1. Two Rooks.
2. Queen (with the aid of the King).
3. Rook (with the aid of the King).
4. Two Bishops (with the aid of the King).
5. Knight and Bishop (with the aid of the King).
6. Three Knights (with the aid of the King).

It follows that if you have one of the above forces together with some additional material the mate is all the easier.

Cases 5 and 6 are so exceedingly rare in practice (in forty years experience of chess I have failed to observe a single example) that I have not thought them worth the space.

THE OPPOSITION

By the nature of the rules the Kings are unable to approach each other directly, but must always stand, at the nearest, one square apart.

Nevertheless, they can effectively block each other's way and prevent each other from reaching vital squares. When one side (side A) is facing the other (side B) and forces the opposing King to move so that side A can gain a square on the intervening rank or file, then that side (A) is said to have the opposition. This opposition is of three types, vertical, as in Diagram 20, horizontal, as in Diagram 21, and diagonal, as in Diagram 22.

In Diagram 20 you will observe that both sides block each

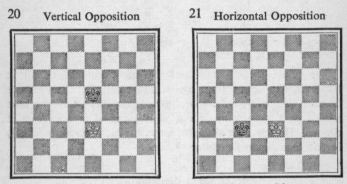

20   Vertical Opposition   21   Horizontal Opposition

The side *not* having the move has the opposition

other's way to White's fourth rank. If it is Black's turn to move – i.e. if White has the opposition, then the Black King must give way, e.g. if *1.* .... K – B4; *2.* K – Q4, or if *1.* .... K – Q4; *2.* K – B4.

In Diagram 21 it is the Q file that is no-man's-land. If it is White's move – i.e. if Black has the opposition, then the Black King can get there. *1.* K – K4, K – Q7; or *1.* K – K2, K – Q5.

Note that when a player does gain a footing on the intervening rank or file he must surrender the opposition in return for this concession, and this shows how delicate is the balance of power in matters of opposition.

The diagonal opposition can be converted into horizontal or vertical opposition by one move and then the rank-or-file gaining

process becomes operative, e.g. in Diagram 22 if Black plays
1. .... K—Q4; *2.* K—Q3 gains the vertical opposition for
White. Or should it be White's turn to play then *1.* K—K4,
K—B5; gives Black the horizontal opposition.

Diagonal Opposition

22

The side *not* having the move has the opposition

This question of the opposition becomes especially important
when dealing with King-and-Pawn endings.

KING-AND-PAWN ENDINGS

The Pawn, though the humblest figure on the board at the
beginning and for a long time in the game, is particularly important in the ending by virtue of its capacity for changing into a
Queen (or other piece) on reaching the eighth rank.

Indeed, next to administering mate one's most vital objective
in the game is to queen a Pawn. This nearly always takes prime
place in the ending when lines have been cleared by exchanges
and the Pawn can obtain a free run home. It equally follows that
the side against whom the Pawn is queening must strive with all
his might and main to prevent this. When only King and Pawns
are left it falls to the King to do the job.

First

One must work out whether the King is within range of the queening square and can arrive in time to stop the Pawn. In Diagram 23 whether the Black King is on the move or not it

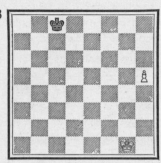

Black cannot stop the Pawn from queening

cannot hope to prevent the White Pawn from queening. In three moves the White Pawn will queen; in three moves the Black King can only reach KB1.

In Diagram 24, on the other hand, whether Black has the

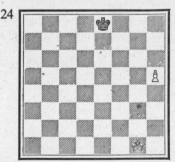

Black can stop the Pawn from queening

move or not, he is still in time to stop the Pawn from queening since now he needs only two moves to stop the White Pawn.

30

A simple method of discovering whether you can stop a Pawn or not is to envisage a square figure formed by the number of squares from the Pawn to the queening square and see if the King comes within the area of this figure. If it is your opponent's turn to move you must be within the square; if it is your turn to move then you only need to be on the point of entering the square as in Diagram 25.

The queening quadrate

25

Black to move can enter the square

Second

One must discover whether, even if the King is within range, the opponent can, by the use of the opposition, still force his Pawn home with the aid of his King.

KING AND TWO PAWNS AGAINST KING

This presents no difficulty for the side with the more material. Two united Pawns are very powerful and the opposing King cannot stop them. Take the position in Diagram 26 with White to play.

    1. K – K3   K – Q2

He cannot play *1.* .... K × P; because of *2.* P – Q7, and the King cannot get back to stop the Pawn. Bear this idea well in mind as it often occurs in some form or other in the endings.

2. K – Q4	K – K3
3. K – K4	K – Q2
4. K – Q5	K – Q1
5. K – B6	

5. P – K6, will also win, but as a general rule it is best to advance your King as much as possible and hold your Pawn moves in reserve.

5.	K – B1

If *5. .... K – K1 ; 6. K – B7*, and the QP marches on.

6. P – Q7 ch	K – Q1
7. P – K6	

Not *7. K – Q6*, when it is stalemate.

7.	K – K2
8. K – B7, and the QP queens.	

This was easy, and the strength of two united passed Pawns can be gauged from the fact that when they are on the sixth rank they are too much even for a Rook. See Diagram 27. (A passed

26

27

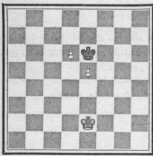

White to play and win

Two Pawns on sixth win against the Rook

Pawn is one that has no enemy Pawn in the file in front of it or on the adjacent files.)

Without the aid of the King (which is not in the queening

quadrate) the Black Rook cannot stop one of the White Pawns from queening. If *1.* .... R—Kt1; *2.* P—R7, R×P; *3.* P—R8 =Q ch, K—B2; *4.* Q—R7 ch, winning the Rook. Similarly if *1.* .... R—R1; *2.* P—Kt7, R×P; *3.* P—Kt8=Q ch, K—B2; *4.* Q—Kt7 ch. If *1.* .... R—Q3; *2.* P—Kt7, R—Kt3; *3.* P—R7, R×P; *4.* P—R8=Q ch. Finally if *1.* .... R—Q8 ch; *2.* K—B2, R—QKt8; *3.* P—R7, R×P; *4.* P—R8=Q ch.

The win with two separate Pawns against the King also is easy enough and the farther the Pawns are away from each other the worse it is for the solitary King. In the extreme case (Diagram 28) White can win without using his own King at all.

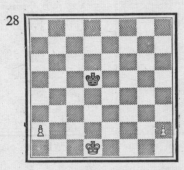

28

Two separate Pawns win

1. P—KR4	K—K4
2. P—R4	K—B4
3. P—QR5	K—Kt5
4. P—R6, and White queens his QRP.	

KING AND ONE PAWN AGAINST KING

This is the most common and important type of Pawn ending and it is therefore essential to know just how to play it. The greatest possible use must be made of the King and of its most powerful weapon, the opposition; whilst one should be very sparing of committal Pawn moves.

The two typical final winning positions are as in Diagrams 29 and 30.

In Diagram 29 White plays *1*. P—Q7 and Black must reply *1*. .... K—K2; when *2*. K—B7, forces the Pawn home. Note that if it were Black's turn to move he could draw by *1*. .... K—B1; (gaining the opposition) *2*. P—Q7 ch, K—Q1; *3*. K—K6, stalemate.

In Diagram 30 White wins by *1*. K—B7, when the QP cannot

29   30

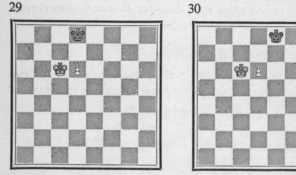

Typical winning positions: White to play

be stopped. He must not play *1*. P—Q7 ch, K—Q1; *2*. K—Q6, stalemate – a simple illustration of the principle given above – but move the King rather than the Pawn.

Such winning positions can always be achieved when White (assuming him to be the side with the more material) has the opposition and *his King is at least one square in front of the Pawn.* The point is that White needs a spare move with his Pawn in order to force back the Black King.

See Diagram 31. If Black plays

1.	K—B3
2. K—K5	K—B4

If *2*. .... K—Q2; *3*. K—Q5, and White has gained further ground.

34

3. P—Q4 ch	K—B3
4. K—K6	

Essential. White must regain the opposition and not give check; for if 4. P—Q5 ch, K—Q2; 5. P—Q6, K—Q1; 6. K—K6, K—K1; 7. P—Q7 ch, K—Q1; 8. K—Q6, stalemate.

4.	K—B2
5. P—Q5	K—Q1
6. K—Q6	

Not 6. P—Q6, when K—K1 draws as above – once again White must get the opposition.

6.	K—K1

7. K—B7, and the QP goes through.

This rule does not apply when the Pawn is a Rook's Pawn since the opponent's King can never be edged out of the corner (Diagram 32).

31

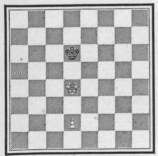

Black to play, White wins

32

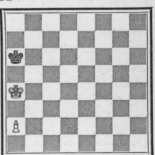

Draw with either side to play

1.	K—R2
2. K—R5	K—R1
3. K—R6	K—Kt1
4. P—R4	K—R1
5. P—R5	K—Kt1

6. K—Kt6	K—R1
7. P—R6	K—Kt1
8. P—R7 ch	K—R1
9. K—R6, stalemate.	

35

The Rook's Pawn is doubly unfortunate, for the weaker side can also force a draw even if his King is not in the corner (Diagram 33).

1. P–R5	K–B2	*4.* K–R8	K–B1
2. K–R7	K–B1	*5.* P–R7	K–B2; stale-
3. P–R6	K–B2		mate.

33

Draw no matter who is to move

34

White to play and win

The general rule for the defending side in all King and single Pawn endings is *keep the King in front of the opposing King* (i.e. retain the opposition), or, if this is not possible, *directly in front of the Pawn.*

KING AND TWO PAWNS AGAINST
KING AND ONE PAWN

This is another common ending and usually (though not always) results in a win for the side with the two Pawns.

Again the question of the opposition is all-important. This comes out clearest in the typical position in Diagram 34. White tries to penetrate with his King.

    1. K – B6   K – Q1

If *1.* .... K–K1; *2.* K–K6 (gaining the opposition, 2. .... K–Q1; *3.* P–Q7.

2. P — Q7

The only way. If 2. K — K6, K — K1; 3. P — Q7 ch, K — Q1;
4. K — Q6, stalemate.

2.	K × P	7. K — Q7	K — Kt1
3. K — B7	K — Q1	8. K × P	K — B1
4. K — K6	K — B2	9. K — Q6	K — Q1
5. K — K7	K — B1	10. P — B6	K — B1
6. K — Q6	K — Kt2	11. P — B7 and wins.	

This sort of ending often occurs in practical play; cf. the ending I had in the London International Tournament, 1946 (Diagram 35).

35　　　Black (Pomar)　　　36

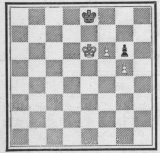
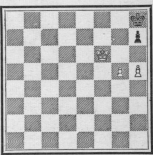

White (Golombek) to play　　　White to play and Black
　　　and win　　　　　　　　to draw

1. P — B7 ch	K — B1	6. K — B6	K — R2
2. K — Q7	K × P	7. K — B7	K — R1
3. K — Q6	K — B1	8. K × P	K — Kt1
4. K — K6	K — Kt2	9. K — R6	K — R1
5. K — K7	K — R1	10. P — Kt6	resigns.

The occasions when two Pawns do not win against one usually involve the existence of Rook Pawns. In Diagram 36 White can neither winkle the Black King out of the corner nor force his Pawn on to queen. 1. P — Kt6, P — R3; 2. P — Kt7 ch, K — Kt1;

and there is no point in White's giving up his KtP to win the RP as the ending with R Pawns is always drawn, as pointed out on page 35.

EQUAL PAWNS

It does not always follow that with the same number of Pawns on each side the game is drawn, and an instructive example is Diagram 37.

Break-through

37

White to play and win

White wins by *1.* P—Kt5, BP×P; *2.* P—R5, P×RP; *3.* P—B5, P—R5; *4.* P—B6, P—R6; *5.* P—B7, P—R7; *6.* P—B8=Q ch.

Or Black may play *1.* .... RP×P; *2.* P—B5, P×BP; *3.* P—R5, and White queens with check first.

Keep this idea of a break-through by a sacrifice always in mind as it frequently is a winning motif in the ending.

CHAPTER 3

THE OPENINGS

IN order to obtain any advantage – indeed, in order to play at all – it is essential to get one's pieces out as soon as possible. It is of no use trying to attack the enemy with just one piece; all that then happens is that he concentrates on the single piece with all his forces and destroys it or else makes it retreat with loss of time.

There are many types of opening in chess, but all obey the fundamental rule of *developing the pieces from the back rank as soon as possible*.

One word of warning: do not bring out your Queen too early in the game. It is too valuable a piece to expose to the attack of lesser forces and you will only lose time and have to retreat if you make a premature sortie with the Queen.

The general order of development is as follows:

1. Advance a Pawn so as to afford your pieces lines on which to develop.
2. Bring out the Knights. These are slow-stepping pieces that work best away from the back ranks or side files; but once established in the centre they can be very powerful.
3. Develop the Bishops. Their ideal station is side by side so as to provide a blast line against the enemy position.
4. Castle. This puts the King in a safe position and is the first step in developing the Rooks.
5. Centralize the Rooks and improve the position of the Queen.

Keeping this order in mind let us see how it is borne out in the standard openings.

THE FOUR KNIGHTS' GAME

1. P—K4

Opening a diagonal for the K Bishop and the Queen and attacking the squares Q5 and KB5.

1. ....   P—K4

Black imitates White with the same idea in mind.

2. Kt—KB3

Not merely bringing the Knight nearer the centre of operations but also attacking a Pawn. A golden rule – *always develop with attack if possible*; it speeds up development and harasses the enemy.

2. ....   Kt—QB3

He defends the Pawn and at the same time brings out a Knight.

3. Kt—B3   Kt—B3
4. B—Kt5

The Knights having been developed, White now brings out his Bishop to a square where it apparently threatens to win a Pawn by *5.* B × Kt, followed by *6.* Kt × P. At the same time the way is cleared for castling. Note that the method of development is strictly in accordance with the order outlined above.

4. ....   B—Kt5

The Best System of Defence is Counter-attack. To defend his Pawn by P—Q3 would shut in his K Bishop and allow White to increase his initiative by *5.* P—Q4. He does not fear *5.* B × Kt, QP × B; (it is usually better, when recapturing, to take off in such a fashion that one's Pawns get nearer the centre; but here it is preferable to take off with the QP rather than the KtP since Black develops both his Q Bishop and Queen at one fell swoop). *6.* Kt × P, because of Q—K2 and in view of the double attack on his Knight and KP White must return the Pawn.

5. O—O   O—O

Both Kings are tucked away in the corner for safety and the Rooks are moved nearer the centre files.

6. P — Q3

Opening the way for his QB and threatening in reality this time to win the KP. Again he cannot win and hold on to the KP here, for if *6.* B × Kt, QP × B; *7.* Kt × P, R — K1; (it is preferable to bring the Rook into play rather than the Queen at this stage) *8.* Kt — Q3, B × Kt; *9.* either P × B, Kt × P; and Black has regained his Pawn with a good game.

6. . . . .   P — Q3

7. B — Kt5

An uncomfortable move for Black to face since now his Knight is pinned down to the square KB3. This pin by a Bishop on a Knight is a very common feature of opening and middle game play.

7. . . . .   B × Kt

A necessary exchange, since White was threatening Kt — Q5 followed by Kt × Kt ch when Black has to break up the Pawns in front of his King by P × B, leaving his King thus open to attack.

8. P × B   Q — K2

38

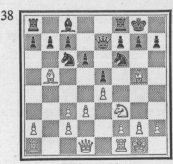

White to play

Why this move? There are three reasons:

1. The Queen is nearer the centre on K2, i.e. it is developed and from this square can be much more active than on its original place. Indeed in a large number of openings the

best square for the Queen is K2, so that one might term, K2 the natural middle-game position for the Queen.

2. White is eventually going to attack Black's centre pawn by P—Q4, and Black therefore gives it additional support with his Queen.

3. A square is vacated for the QKt, which he proposes to centralize still further by Kt—Q1 and Kt—K3 (this, by the way, attacks the pinning Bishop).

    9. R—K1

Centralization of the Rook; additional defence of the KP so as to prepare for P—Q4, and bringing the Rook on to a line where it attacks, however indirectly, the enemy Queen. *Always try to place your Rook opposite the opponent's Queen.* It pays to threaten a piece of greater value by a piece of lesser calibre.

    9. ....   Kt—Q1

The consequent point of Black's previous move. As Black you will find it essential to form *a logical plan of defence and counter-attack.*

    10. P—Q4

Tempting Black to exchange Pawns when, after *10.* .... P×P; *11.* P×P, White would possess greater control of the centre and already be threatening to win a piece by P—K5.

    10. ....   B—Kt5

39

White to play. The position is level

and the position is approximately level. White's Pawns are not so well placed as Black's (the doubled Pawns on the QB file can well prove a handicap at a later stage in the game); but he enjoys command of greater space. He will complete his development by playing QR–Kt1 and moving his Bishop back to Q3, whilst Black will play P–B3 and Kt–K3.

THE SCOTCH GAME

This is one of the simplest of all openings and from this point of view very suitable for the beginner. Its main idea is *violent attack on the centre*. The name is derived from its successful use by the Edinburgh Chess Club in a correspondence game against London as long ago as 1824.

1.	P–K4	P–K4
2.	Kt–KB3	Kt–QB3
3.	P–Q4	

A vigorous move that forces Black to exchange Pawns.

3.	....	P × P

Best – two common mistakes by the inexperienced are (*a*) 3. .... P–Q3; 4. P × P, Kt × P; 5. Kt × Kt, P × Kt; 6. Q × Q ch, K × Q; 7. B–QB4, when Black has not only lost the right to Castle but must waste a move protecting his KBP; and (*b*) 3. .... Kt × P; 4. Kt × Kt, P × Kt; 5. Q × P, and, despite the exchanges which usually tend to favour the defending party, White has an advantage due to the fine position of his Queen.

4.	Kt × P	Kt–B3

Black can also play *4.* .... B–B4; *5.* B–K3, Q–B3; *6.* P–QB3, KKt–K2; with an equal game.

5.	Kt–QB3	B–Kt5

The correct defence, which consists in counter-attack on White's KP.

6.	Kt × Kt	

He wants to defend his KP by B–Q3 and must therefore exchange Kts first.

6. ....   KtP × Kt

A bad mistake would be *6. .... QP × Kt; 7. Q × Q ch,
K × Q; 8. B − KKt5*, and White threatens to win a piece by
9. P − K5.

7. B − Q3   P − Q4!

(Note : != good move and ?= bad move.)

*In all openings where White has commenced 1. P − K4, and
Black can attain P − Q4 without disadvantage he has solved most
of his defensive problems.*

8. P × P   P × P
9. O − O   O − O

In view of the open K file and the possible danger to either
King both sides hasten to castle. Moral − *when there are early
exchanges in the centre it is essential to castle quickly.*

10. B − KKt5

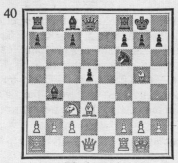

Black to play

A dangerous attacking move which strikes at Black's QP.
There are two threats : (1) *11. B × Kt, Q × B; 12. Kt × P, Q × P;
13. R − Kt1*, winning the Bishop, or (2) *11. Kt × P, Q × Kt;
12. B × Kt, P × B; 13. B × P ch*, winning the Queen.

10. ....   B − K3

44

Supporting the vital point Q4 against which White's plan has been directed.

> *11.* Q−B3

Preparing to bring the QR over to Q1 or K1 and threatening to double Black's Pawn on the KB file.

> *11.* ....   B−K2
> *12.* QR−K1   R−Kt1

and the game is level.

THE SCOTCH GAMBIT

> *1.* P−K4   P−K4
> *2.* Kt−KB3   Kt−QB3
> *3.* P−Q4   P×P

So far as in the Scotch Game; now White sacrifices a Pawn in return for an advantage in position and development (which is what is meant by the term 'Gambit').

> *4.* B−QB4   B−B4
> *5.* P−B3

41

Black to play

Forcing Black to take some notice of White's sacrificial intentions. *5.* Kt−Kt5, attacking Black on his weakest point, KB2, is open to the fundamental objection of waste of time in development – *do not move a piece twice early in the opening*. Black can reply 5. .... Kt–R3; (not 5. .... Kt–K4; which merely duplicates White's error in moving a piece twice) and if 6. Kt×BP, Kt×Kt; 7. B×Kt ch, K×B; 8. Q–R5 ch, P–Kt3; 9. Q×B, P–Q4; 10. P×P, R–K1 ch; 11. K–Q1, R–K4; with the better game for Black.

5.	P×P

Or Black can prudently decline the offer by 5. .... P–Q6.

6. Kt×P

Black has an equal game after 6. B×P ch, K×B; 7. Q–Q5 ch, K–B1; 8. Q×B ch, Q–K2; 9. Q×Q ch, KKt×Q.

6.	P–Q3
7. Q–Kt3	Q–Q2

Both Q–K2 and Q–B3 would be bad because of 8. Kt–Q5.

8. Kt–Q5

White must reluctantly move a piece twice since Black was threatening to disturb his game by 8. ....Kt–R4.

8.	KKt–K2

Kt–R4 would not do now since 9. Q–B3 would hit both the Kt and KKt7.

9. Q–B3	O–O

Black correctly continues his development. 9. .... Kt×Kt; would be all very well if White replied either 10. P×Kt, or B×Kt since Black can then win the Queen by 10. .... B–Kt5; but White has the powerful rejoinder 10. Q×P.

10. O–O	Kt×Kt
11. P×Kt	Kt–K4

It is best for Black to return the Pawn so as to hold up White's attack. If 11. .... Kt–K2; 12. P–QKt4, B–Kt3; 13. B–Kt2, and White has a very strong attack.

12. Kt×Kt	P×Kt
13. Q×P	B–Q3

with a level game.

THE GIUOCO PIANO

1. P—K4	P—K4
2. Kt—KB3	Kt—QB3
3. B—B4	

This venerable opening which was played as long ago as the fifteenth century derives its Italian name (meaning slow or mild game) from the contrast it offers to the various gambit openings; but, as a matter of fact, it can be as violent as the most perturbed of all these openings.

Observe that the Bishop strikes at Black's *weakest point, KB2.*

3.	B—B4
4. P—B3	

This move enhances the action of the Queen (enabling it to dash out to Kt3 when the occasion demands) but this is not its chief purpose. The idea is to prepare to strike at the centre by P—Q4. If Black can then be induced to reply P × P White will recapture with the Pawn and so command the centre. The command of the centre is an all-important aim in the opening and one might say that *all openings are good in so far as they are concerned with the control of the centre.*

Why is the centre so important? Because it is from the centre that your pieces can best attack the enemy; because if you control the centre you automatically control more ground than your opponent, who will consequently find himself confined to a constricted space where his pieces have much less effect. In short, *he who commands the centre commands the game.* See Diagram 42.

Black now has to choose between two main lines. He can allow White to achieve his aim in the centre and play *4.* .... Kt—B3; *5.* P—Q4, P × P; *6.* P × P, B—Kt5 ch; *7.* Kt—B3, Kt × KP; *8.* O—O, B × Kt; *9.* P—Q5, B—B3; *10.* R—K1, Kt—K2; *11.* R × Kt, when theoretically the game is level, but in practice White has nearly always done better than Black. Or else he can play to maintain the centre by

4.	B—Kt3

So that when White's Pawn comes to Q4, Black will be under no compulsion to exchange.

5. P—Q4   Q—K2

42

Black to play

He concentrates his pieces on K4 so as to maintain his control there. Pawn moves are bad, e.g. 5. .... P—Q3; 6. P×P, P×P; (or 6. .... Kt×P; 7. Kt×Kt, P×Kt; 8. B×P ch, winning a Pawn) 7. Q×Q ch, and now Black must lose either the KBP or the KP; whilst 5. .... P—B3 means that Black will be unable to castle.

6. O—O   P—Q3
7. P—KR3

In order to prevent Black from playing B—Kt5 when White would have difficulty in defending his Q4.

7. ....   Kt—B3
8. R—K1

Defending the KP and placing the Rook opposite the Black Queen.

8. ....   O—O
9. Kt—R3

Normally placing Kts on R3 is not to be recommended, but here the move is quite powerful. In any case it cannot go to Q2 because of the pressure Black exerts on White's QP. From R3 the Knight can be centralized eventually to K3 with considerable effect.

43

Black to play

The position is approximately even but on the whole one prefers White's chances as he has more attacking possibilities.

A game Rossolimo–Euwe, Beverwijk, 1950, now continued *9.* .... Kt – Q1; *10.* B – B1, Kt – Q2; *11.* Kt – B4, P – KB3; *12.* P – QR4, P – QR3; *13.* Kt × B, Kt × Kt; *14.* P – QKt3, with some advantage to White.

KING'S GAMBIT

1. P – K4	P – K4
2. P – KB4	

Not often seen nowadays but perhaps the most colourful of all openings and one which has produced more brilliant games than any other. White has three main reasons for offering up a Pawn. (1) To gain control of the centre. (2) To break through to his opponent's KB2 with a mating attack. (3) To gain development.

Often as White you may find it necessary to sacrifice further Pawns to speed up your development, and here remember that *a Pawn sacrifice is worth while if it results in the gain of three moves.*

2. ....   P × P

Black may also refuse to accept the gambit by 2. .... B—B4; or by counter-attacking with 2. .... P—Q4.

3. Kt—KB3

A developing move that also has the advantage of preventing Q—R5 ch. Against 3. B—B4, Black can play 3. .... P—Q4 with a good game.

3. ....   P—KKt4

Black decides to cling on to his Pawn. He has two other main lines at his disposal: (1) 3. .... P—Q4; when White should play 4. P × P, and (2) 3. .... B—K2; to which White's best reply is 4. B—B4.

4. P—KR4

Undermining the basis of Black's Pawn structure. He could also play 4. B—B4, P—Kt5; 5. O—O (the Muzio Gambit) sacrificing a whole piece for a strong attack the soundness of which is still a vexed question.

4. ....   P—Kt5
5. Kt—K5

The Kieseritzky Gambit. Weaker is the Allgaier Gambit 5. Kt—Kt5, P—KR3; 6. Kt × P, when White's attack is not worth the material sacrificed.

This is an excellent example of the superiority of centralization. On K5 the White Kt not only strikes at Black's weak points on KB2 and KKt5 but can also be manoeuvred to strong central positions on Q3 and KB4. See Diagram 44.

5. ....   Kt—KB3

Black's best defence. If 5. .... P—Q3; 6. Kt × KtP, and if 5. .... P—Q4; 6. P—Q4! are good for White.

6. P—Q4!

It is much better to continue his development and place a Pawn in the centre rather than take off a Pawn himself by Kt × KtP.

Black to play

The Centralized Knight

6.	P – Q3
7. Kt – Q3	Kt × P
8. B × P	

White is still a Pawn down, but in return he has the better development and has succeeded in his objective of opening up the KB file for attack.

8.	Q – K2

An aggressive defence is always preferable to passive lines. He threatens to win the Queen by discovering check with the Kt to B6.

9. Q – K2	B – Kt2
10. P – B3	P – KR4
11. Kt – Q2	

Note that even though this involves the exchange of Queens White increases his advantage in development and his attack does not slacken.

11.	Kt × Kt

11. .... P – Q4; 12. Kt × Kt, P × Kt; 13. Kt – K5, or 11. .... P – KB4; 12. B – Kt5, Kt × B; 13. Q × Q ch, K × Q; 14. P × Kt, Kt – B3; 15. Kt – B4 are both favourable to White.

12. K × Kt	Q × Q ch

He must exchange Queens as otherwise White plays Q—B2 with the threat of R—K1.

13.	B × Q	B—B4
14.	KR—KB1	Kt—B3
15.	B—Kt5	B—Kt3
16.	Kt—B4	

and though Black is still a Pawn up he has much the worse position.

Black to play

45

The game might continue 16. .... O—O; 17. B—Q3, B × B; 18. Kt × B, P—B3; 19. B—K3, K—B2; 20. Kt—B4, R—R1; 21. Kt—Q5, QR—QB1; 22. B—Kt5, when White regains his Pawn with considerable advantage.

THE RUY LOPEZ

1.	P—K4	P—K4
2.	Kt—KB3	Kt—QB3
3.	B—Kt5	

Another old opening which is however still justly popular today since it is one of the strongest of all. It derives its name from a celebrated Spanish player of the sixteenth century. Its point is that White indirectly attacks Black's K4 (an eventual threat of B × Kt and Kt × P always hovers over Black's head) and so tries to gain mastery of the centre. The Bishop move has other advantages. It dissuades Black from advancing his QP owing to the prospective pin on the Kt and so interferes with Black's natural means of developing his Q side. Finally it prepares for a rapid K-side castling.

    3. ....   P — QR3

So that, when and if the Bishop retreats to R4, he can hold in reserve the possibility of driving back the Bishop altogether by P — QKt4.

    4. B — R4

White cannot as yet win the KP by *4.* B × Kt, QP × B; *5.* Kt × P, because of *5.* .... Q — Q5.

    4. ....   Kt — B3

Counter-attack against White's own KP.

    5. O — O

But White can also ignore this attack.

    5. ....   B — K2

5. .... Kt × P; leads to quite a different type of game of much more open character. (See later Ch. 8, p. 178.)

    6. R — K1

Black was now threatening to capture and retain the KP. With the text White in turn threatens to play *7.* B × Kt, QP × B; *8.* Kt × P, when Q — Q5 will no longer work because of *9.* Kt — KB3.

    6. ....   P — QKt4
    7. B — Kt3   P — Q3

See Diagram 46.

Aggressive players might prefer the Marshall attack here by *7.* .... O — O; *8.* P — B3, P — Q4; *9.* P × P, Kt × P; *10.* Kt × P, Kt × Kt; *11.* R × Kt, Kt — B3; but White can weather the storm by *12.* R — K1, B — Q3; *13.* P — KR3, Kt — Kt5; *14.* Q — B3, (not *14.* P × Kt, Q — R5; with a winning attack), *14.* .... Q — R5; *15.* P — Q4, Kt × P; *16.* R — K2, (Black wins after *16.* Q × Kt, B — R7 ch; *17.* K — B1, B — Kt6;) *16.* .... B — KKt5; *17.* P × B, B — R7 ch; *18.* K — B1, B — Kt6; *19.* R × Kt, as in the game Capablanca–Marshall, New York, 1918, when White had the advantage.

46

White to play

8. P – B3

Preparing to build up a Pawn centre by P – Q4 and also giving the Bishop a square of retreat on B2.

8. ....   O – O

9. P – KR3

Preventing B – Kt5 which is what Black would do if White played *9.* P – Q4, at once.

9. ....   Kt – QR4

Whilst it is not normally good to place a Kt on the R file (where its field of action is halved) here the move is part of a plan of counter-attack on the Q side. In this main line of the Ruy Lopez the plans of campaign for White and Black are clearly contrasted: White tries to gain control of the centre and inaugurate a K-side attack, whereas Black endeavours to maintain his own central position whilst counter-attacking on the Q side.

10. B – B2

At the moment this Bishop looks inoffensive, but White always has hopes of an attack along the diagonal QKt1 – KR7.

10. ....   P – B4

11. P – Q4   Q – B2

Thus Black maintains his centre Pawn on K4.

12. QKt—Q2

This Kt will be brought over to the K side to reinforce White's attack there.

47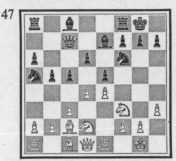

Black to play

12. ....   BP × P

Black is at an important crossroads here. The text move takes advantage of the presence of the Q on the QB file to get pressure along that line. There are four other possibilities:

(*a*) *12.* .... Kt—B3; (so as to induce White to play P—Q5 and release the tension in the centre) *13.* P—Q5, Kt—Q1; *14.* P—QR4, R—Kt1; *15.* P—B4, B—Q2; with equal chances.

(*b*) *12.* .... B—Kt2; *13.* P—Q5, when Black's QB is not well placed.

(*c*) *12.* .... B—Q2; *13.* Kt—B1, QR—B1; *14.* P × KP, P × P; *15.* B—KKt5, KR—Q1; *16.* Q—K2, B—K3; *17.* Kt—K3, and White has rather the better position as his Kts are more centralized.

(*d*) *12.* .... Kt—Q2; *13.* Kt—B1, Kt—Kt3; *14.* Kt—K3, P—B3; *15.* P—QKt3, Kt—B3; *16.* P—Q5, Kt—Q1; and again White has the better chances as he can build up a K-side attack by K—R2, P—KKt4, and R—KKt1, whilst Black has little or no counter on the Q side.

13. P × P	Kt — B3	*17.* B — Kt1	B — Q2
14. Kt — Kt3	P — QR4	*18.* P — R3	Kt — B3
15. B — K3	P — R5	*19.* B — Q3	QR — Kt1
16. Kt(Kt3) — Q2	Kt — QKt5	*20.* P — QKt4	

And White has the better game; if Black plays P × P *e.p.* then *21.* Q × P, leaves Black with a weak Pawn on Kt4; whilst if he refrains from capturing the Pawn then he has no chance of countering on the Q side.

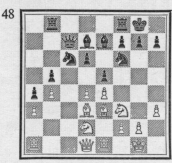

48

Black to play

THE QUEEN'S GAMBIT

1. P — Q4

The most frequently played of all opening moves and one which poses to Black quite a different set of problems from *1.* P — K4.

1. ....　　　　　　　　　P — Q4

2. P — QB4

White has three aims with this move:

(*a*) To lure a Pawn away from the centre.

(*b*) To bring pressure to bear on the QP if aim (*a*) has not been achieved.

(*c*) To attack along the QB file and eventually gain control of it.

2. ....　　　　　　　　　P — K3

49

White to play

The natural way of defending the centre. He can also defend it by 2. .... P—QB3; but not by 2. .... Kt—KB3; which loses time after 3. P×P, Kt×P; 4. P—K4, or 3. .... Q×P; 4. Kt—QB3.

Acceptance of the gambit is quite playable; but not with the idea of retaining the Pawn. For if 2. .... P×P; 3. Kt—KB3, P—QKt4; 4. P—K3, P—QB3; 5. P—QR4, B—Kt2; 6. P×P, P×P; 7. P—QKt3, Q—B1; 8. P×P, P×P; 9. Q—R4 ch, and White regains his Pawn with the better game.

So Black, if he wishes to play the Queen's Gambit Accepted, should continue 2. .... P×P; 3. Kt—KB3, Kt—KB3; 4. P—K3, P—K3; 5. B×P, P—B4; 6. O—O, P—QR3; 7. Q—K2, Kt—B3; 8. R—Q1, P—QKt4; 9. B—Kt3, P—B5; 10. B—B2, Kt—QKt5; 11. P—K4, Kt×B; 12. Q×Kt, B—Kt2; with about a level game. White has command of the centre and can thrust forward with P—Q5, but Black has some compensation in the possession of two Bishops.

    3. Kt—QB3   Kt—KB3
    4. B—Kt5

Bringing fresh pressure to bear on the QP (compare the Bishop manoeuvre in the Ruy Lopez). He threatens 5. B×Kt. Q×B; 6. P×P, P×P; 7. Kt×P.

    4. ....   B—K2

Black can also play *4.* .... QKt−Q2; for if then *5.* P×P, P×P; *6.* Kt×P?, Kt×Kt!; *7.* B×Q, B−Kt5 ch; *8.* Q−Q2, B×Q ch; *9.* K×B, K×B; and Black wins a piece.

5. P−K3	O−O
6. Kt−B3	QKt−Q2

Another defence is *6.* .... Kt−K5; (Lasker's Defence), or Black may first play *6.* .... P−KR3; *7.* B−R4, Kt−K5; *8.* B×B, Q×B; *9.* P×P, Kt×Kt; *10.* P×Kt, P×P; *11.* Q−Kt3, Q−Q3; *12.* P−B4, P×P; *13.* B×P, Kt−B3; *14.* Q−Kt2, B−Kt5; *15.* O−O, B×Kt; *16.* P×B, Q−B3; *17.* B−K2, with equality.

   7. R−B1

In accordance with one of White's main themes – attack along the QB file.

   7. ....   P−B3

Blocking the above-mentioned attack. After *7.* .... P−B4; *8.* QP×P, Q−R4; *9.* P×P, Kt×QP; *10.* B×B, Kt×B; *11.* P−QR3, Q×BP; *12.* Kt−QKt5, White has much the better game.

   8. B−Q3   P×P

Black falls in with White's intentions. He surrenders the centre in order to embark on an exchange manoeuvre.

9. B×P	Kt−Q4	*11.* O−O	Kt×Kt
10. B×B	Q×B	*12.* R×Kt	

If *12.* P×Kt, P−QB4; and Black has a good game.

   12. ....   P−K4

Continuing his policy of exchange and eventually of development of the Q Bishop. The great difficulty for Black in practically all types of Q-Pawn openings is the development of this Bishop. *When Black manages to develop his Q Bishop satisfactorily he has solved the problem of defence in Q-side openings.*

How is White to avoid or thwart (1) over-simplification of the position by frequent exchanges and (2) development of Black's Q Bishop? Many lines have been tried here.

50

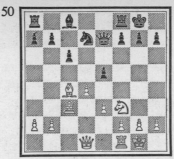

White to play

(a) *13.* P—K4, P×P; *14.* Q×P, Kt—Kt3; *15.* B—Kt3, B—K3; and Black, having developed his QB satisfactorily, stands well.

(b) *13.* Q—B2, P—K5; *14.* Kt—Q2, Kt—B3; and Black will play B—B4 next move with a good game.

(c) *13.* B—Kt3, P—K5; *14.* Kt—Q2, Kt—B3; *15.* Q—Kt1, B—B4; with equality.

(d) *13.* R—K1, P—K5; *14.* Kt—Q2, Kt—B3; with similar lines to those in (b) and (c).

(e) *13.* Q—Kt1, P×P; *14.* P×P, Kt—B3; *15.* R—K1, Q—Q3; *16.* QR—K3, B—Kt5; and though White still has some initiative Black has an adequate defence.

(f) *13.* P—Q5, P—K5; *14.* Kt—Q2, P×P; *15.* B×P, Kt—B3; *16.* B—Kt3, B—Kt5; and Black has again developed his QB with a level game.

Reverting to the position in Diagram 50 we now come to White's most aggressive continuation, which is called the Rubinstein variation after the great Polish master, Akiba Rubinstein, who introduced the line.

13. P×P	Kt×P
14. Kt×Kt	Q×Kt
15. P—B4	

Taking advantage of the position of the Queen to make an

attacking thrust on the K side. In addition the Pawn threatens to go to B5, thereby preventing the development of the Q Bishop.

    15. ....   Q – B3

Best; other Queen moves are inferior. If (*a*) *15.* .... Q – K2; *16.* P – B5, P – QKt4; *17.* B – Kt3, P – Kt5; *18.* P – B6, breaking up Black's K side and giving White a strong attack.

Of if (*b*) *15.* .... Q – K5; *16.* Q – K2, B – B4; *17.* P – KKt4, B – K3; *18.* B – Q3, Q – Kt5; *19* P – QR3, Q – Kt3; *20.* P – B5, B – Q4; *21.* P – B6, P – Kt3; *22.* Q – KB2, KR – K1; *23.* B – Kt1, R – K3; *24.* P – Kt4, QR – K1; *25.* R – K1, Q – Q1; *26.* P – Kt5, with advantage to White.

51

Position after *15.* .... Q – B3
White to play

    16. P – B5

Shutting in the Bishop; Black cannot now play *16.* .... B × P; because of *17.* P – K4, winning the piece.

    16. ....   P – QKt4
    17. B – Q3   P – Kt5
    18. R – QB2   R – Q1
    19. Q – K2   P – QR4

and the game is about even.

CHAPTER 4

THE MIDDLE GAME:
ELEMENTS OF COMBINATION

THE Middle Game is that phase of the game when the players have developed their pieces and left the opening stages. It is a phase when the player is most on his own – when he has to rely more on his own judgement and less on what theorists tell him.

Here practice is more important than preaching, but nevertheless a great deal of the skill in middle-game play can be acquired by following certain basic principles and by becoming acquainted with the various but basic types of combination. The most important principle of all lies in the *forming of a plan that fits in with the nature of the opening already chosen*. Drifting along from move to move merely leads to swift disaster.

Though chess itself is almost infinitely varied and in consequence the plans that can be formed are practically inexhaustible in number, the means by which these plans are carried out and the combinations of moves by which one's ideas are fulfilled fall into set types and are readily learnable.

52

The Pawn Fork

The forceful means of these combinations can be divided into three elements: (1) the Fork, (2) the Pin, (3) Check and all its varieties, simple, discovered, and double – this last being the most powerful of all means.

THE FORK

When a piece is attacking more than one piece at the same time we say that it is forking them. This is clearly an embarrassing situation for the side attacked, since no matter what he does one at least of his pieces is still liable to be captured on the following move. In Diagram 52 where the Pawn forks the Rooks one of

The Knight Fork

The Bishop Fork

these can be captured no matter which side has the move. Similarly in Diagram 53 either Queen or Rook will fall to the Knight. The Bishop will capture a Rook in Diagram 54; Black loses his Queen in Diagram 55 and a Rook will be taken by the Queen in Diagram 56.

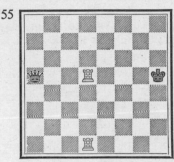

The Rook Fork

The Queen Fork

The fork is a powerful weapon for gaining material and one that is generally more powerful when a piece of lesser value is attacking two pieces of greater value. By far the most frequent type of fork is that with the Knight. Players of all categories –

from beginners to masters – fall victim to this and a well-known type is the so-called family fork where the Knight forks Queen, Rook, and King with, as can well be imagined, fatal results.

Here are three examples; not of the family fork, but of more subtle yet colourful character. Diagram 57 is from a game in the 1952 Women's Championship Candidate Tournament at Moscow. At first glance White seems to have no fork available, but it is there all the same owing to the pressure White exerts along the KB file. White played Kt–K8 ch, whereupon Black

Black (E. Keller)

57

White (E. Bikova) to play

Black (Gligoric)

58

White (Nedeljkovic) to play, Yugoslav Championship, 1952

resigned. For if *1.* .... R × Kt; *2.* Q × P ch, K − R3; *3.* Q × R, with an easy win.

Diagram 58 is rather more subtle but the forking motif is still there. Play went *49.* R × B ch, K × R; *50.* P − R7, resigns. Black cannot stop the Pawn from queening. If *50.* .... K − Kt2; *51.* Kt − R5 ch, forking King and Rook.

Diagram 59 contains a dazzling series of forks. Apparently White cannot move the Knight on K6 without losing the Queen but he plays *53.* Kt − B5!, R − K2; (if *53.* .... Q × Q; *54.* Kt × R

Black (Hilse)

59

White (Nimzovitch)
Major A Tournament, Coburg, 1904

ch, and whether the King goes to B1 or R1 White still wins the Queen by the fork *55.* Kt − Kt6 ch) *54.* Q × Q, R × Q; (now comes another fork) *55.* Kt − Q6, R − Kt2; *56.* Kt(B5) × B, R − Kt5; *57.* Kt − B5, R × RP; *58.* Kt − Q3, R − Kt5; *59.* Kt − K8, R × P; *60.* Kt × BP, R × P; *61.* Kt × RP, P − K5; *62.* P − B6, R − R4; *63.* P − B7, R − KB4; *64.* Kt − K5! (the decisive fork − he now threatens *65.* P − B8 = Q ch, R × Q; *66.* Kt − Q7 ch) *64.* .... P − K6; *65.* Kt − Kt3, resigns. The Rook must move and allow White to bring off the fork given in the last note. If *65.* .... P − K7; *66.* Kt × R, P − K8 = Q; *67.* P − B8 = Q ch, K − B2; *68.* Q − B5 ch, K − Kt2;

69. Kt—Q6 ch, K—Kt1; *70.* Q—Kt6 ch, K—R1; *71.* Q—Kt7 mate.

THE PIN

A recurrent theme throughout the game is that of the pin, when a piece is so placed that it prevents an enemy piece from moving because of a hidden attack on a piece of greater value. This idea is a much more permanent process than the preceding one (the

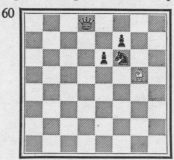

fork) and can hamper the movement of both the enemy pieces concerned. See Diagram 60 where the White Bishop firmly pins the Knight down on the Queen. A still more permanent type of pin is that involving the King as in Diagram 61, or, worse still for Black, as in Diagram 62.

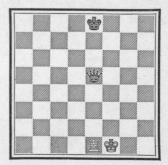

A great danger to be avoided by the pinned side is that the force of the pin may be strengthened by additional attack, more especially by a Pawn as in Diagram 60a where P—K5 wins the Knight for White.

60a

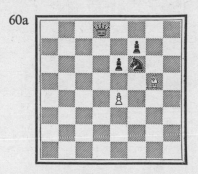

As appears in Diagrams 61 and 62 another common pitfall emerges when one incautiously moves or leaves a piece in line with the King. A further example of this appears in Diagram 63 where Black simply wins the Queen by B—R5.

A combination of the pin and the fork in its clearest form is seen in Diagram 64. This type (or the threat of it) is quite common. If Q × B Black loses his Queen after Kt—B7 ch.

63

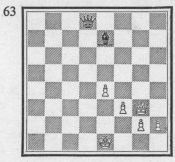

64

The pin may be used to enforce mate in a number of ways. In Diagram 65 Black takes advantage of the pin of the Rook by the Queen to mate by *1.* .... Kt—Kt6 ch; *2.* P×Kt, Q—R6

Black (Soultanbeieff) to play

65

White ('L. Smith')
Hastings Premier Reserves, 1950

mate. In Diagram 66 the influence of a pin is more subtle. White's aim is to force mate on K7 so he plays *1.* R—B8! whereupon Black resigns. For White threatens mate on the move and if *1.* .... R×R; *2.* R×R, B×R; *3.* Q×Q mate or *2.* .... Q×R; *3.* Q—K7 mate; whilst if *1.* .... B×R; *2.* Q×Q mate.

Black (Goldenov)

66

White (Bronstein) to play
Kiev, 1944

Another neat use of the pin to enforce mate or win of material is shown in Diagram 67. White plays Q—B6! and Black resigns as he loses the Bishop on K2. Here there is a double pin on the Bishop, not only legally but through the threat of mate on KB7.

Black (Rossolimo)

67

White (Schmid) to play
Völklingen, 1953

Mate by means of a pin can come quite early in the game. E.g. *1.* P—Q4, Kt—KB3; *2.* P—QB4, P—K4; *3.* P×P, Kt—K5; *4.* Kt—Q2, Kt—B4; *5.* KKt—B3, Kt—B3; *6.* P—QR3, Q—K2; *7.* P—KKt3, P—Q3; *8.* P×P??, Kt—Q6 mate. Or even quicker as in *1.* P—K4, P—QB3; *2.* Kt—QB3, P—Q4; *3.* Kt—B3, P×P; *4.* Kt×P, Kt—B3; *5.* Q—K2, QKt—Q2??; *6.* Kt—Q6 mate. This last game occurred in the Bad Salzbrunn International Tournament 1950 between Keres and Arlamowski.

These two examples show that you must always scent danger when your opponent brings his Queen into line with your King. There is a kind of hierarchy in chess; *always place a piece so that it attacks either directly or indirectly an opposing piece of greater value.* The piece of greatest value is the King. Therefore, place the Queen versus the King, and then the Rook against the Queen, etc.

In addition to the simple example given in 60a the pin can be used in a variety of ways to gain material. In Diagram 68 White played *1.* R—Q1, when Black resigned. For if *1.* .... Q×Q; *2.* R×R ch, followed by P×Q.

Black (Aitken)

White (Yanofsky) to play
Hastings, 1947

In Diagram 69 White has sacrificed a piece to obtain a lasting pin and now brings about a decisive gain in material by *1.* R × Kt, R × R; *2.* R − Q1, O − O; *3.* R × R, B − B3; *4.* R × RP, and wins.

Black (Dr Ed. Lasker)

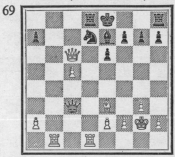

White (Golombek) to play
Hastings, 1953

A multiple type of pin is shown in the final position of the game on Diagram 70 where Black now resigned. The Queen not

Black (Miss Menchik) to play

White (Kan)
Moscow, 1935

only pins down the Pawn on Kt7 but also the Rook on Q2. For if *1*. .... R(Q2)—B2; (or *1*. .... Kt—Kt1;) *2*. B×P, whilst mate follows after *1*. .... R(B1)—B2; *2*. R—K8 ch, K—B2; *3*. Q—K6.

All pins are not so permanent as they may seem. Cf. the variation in the Queen's Gambit given on page 58 or the position in Diagram 71. Now Black played *1*. .... Kt×Kt!; *2*. B×Q,

71 Black (Fairhurst) to play

White (Spencer)
Tenby, 1928

72   Black to play

B—Kt5 ch; *3*. Q—Q2, B×Q ch; *4*. K—Q1, R×B; *5*. P—B3, B—Kt4; and White resigned since a piece was lost. Still more drastic is the following brevity: *1*. P—K4, P—K4; *2*. Kt—KB3, P—Q3; *3*. B—B4, P—KR3; *4*. Kt—B3, B—Kt5?; (a false pin) *5*. Kt×P!, B×Q; *6*. B×P ch, K—K2; *7*. Kt—Q5 mate.

CHECK

The check is not only a means of pursuing the King but also a weapon that can be used to gain material. The point of the combinations involved here is that while the checked side is engaged in dealing with the check, the checker can snatch material.

See Diagram 72 which arises from the moves *1*. P—Q4,

P—Q4; *2.* P—QB4, Kt—KB3; *3.* P×P, Kt×P; *4.* P—K4, Kt—KB3; *5.* B—Q3, now if Black incautiously takes the Pawn by 5. .... Q×P; he loses his Queen after *6.* B—Kt5 ch. Similarly, if in Diagram 73 (a position that may arise out of the

Black to play

73

Queen's Gambit Accepted) Black is so rash as to play *1.* .... Kt×P; then *2.* Kt×Kt, Q×Kt; *3.* B×P ch, and he loses his Queen.

Sometimes this theme is effectively masked by a Pawn as in Diagram 74. Now Black played *17.* .... Kt×QP; and after

Black (Troianescu) to play

74

White (Tolush)
Bucarest, 1953

18. Kt × Kt, R × Kt; *19.* P−K5, Q−B3; *20.* P−B3, Black had to give up the exchange (i.e. lose Rook for Bishop) by *20.* .... R × B; since if the Kt moved White would play B × P ch.

The moral of these last three examples is that you must *keep your pieces in cooperation* – an unsupported piece in enemy territory can so often be snapped up by such combinations.

Even if unmoved a Queen can be in danger when unsupported, as the following trap shows: *1.* P−K4, P−QB4; *2.* Kt−KB3, P−Q3; *3.* P−Q4, P×P; *4.* Kt×P, Kt−KB3; *5.* Kt−QB3, P−KKt3; *6.* P−B4, B−Kt2; *7.* P−K5, P×P; *8.* P×P, Kt−Kt5? (Kt−Kt1 is better) *9.* B−Kt5 ch, K−B1; *10.* Kt−K6 ch, winning the Queen.

Check may also be used to undermine the support of one piece for another. As in Diagram 75 where Black plays *1.* ....

75 Black (Golombek) to play   76 Black (Panov) to play

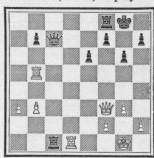

White (Abrahams)
Hastings, 1947

White (Ragosin)
Moscow, 1940

R−B8 ch; and wins a Rook; for if *2.* K−R2, Q×Q; *3.* R×Q, R × R; whilst White loses the Queen after *2.* R × R.

The support is undermined in a different way in Diagram 76. By *25.* .... Q−B3; Black forces White to resign since he wins a Rook. If *26.* Q × Q, R × R ch; and if *26.* Q−Q3 or K2, R × R ch; likewise wins.

Often it will be found that the power of check can force a Pawn through to the queening square. An elementary but important example is Diagram 77 where White has only one winning move:

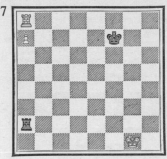

77

White to play

1. R—R8, and if R × P; *2.* R—R7 ch, winning a Rook. A more complicated method of forcing through a Pawn is shown in Diagram 78. This is indeed a most violent tribute to the power of check, play continuing *30.* Q—B4 ch, R × Q; *31.* R × R ch, K—Kt2; *32.* R—Kt8 ch, resigns as White queens a Pawn with mate to follow.

Black (Koska)

78

White (Florian) to play
Brno, 1950

Finally, here is a very old study by Stamma that uses the check as in Diagram 76 but with quite a fresh and different piquancy (Diagram 79). White is threatened with loss of a Rook and with

79

White to play

mate. How is he to meet both threats? By *1*. R—KR5, R×R; *2*. R—R6 ch, K—K4; *3*. R—R5 ch.

DISCOVERED AND DOUBLE CHECK

These two are the deadliest weapons of all and the double check is the atom bomb of the chessboard – nothing can withstand its blast. How effective it is can be seen from Diagram 80

80

White to play

where White mates in two by *1*. R—Kt6 db ch, K×R; *2*. Q—Kt5.

A large number of short games owe their mating finish to the double and discovered check. For instance, the following, played in Basle, 1951: White Kilchsperger, Black Waldhauser: *1*. P—K4, P—K3; *2*. P—Q4, P—Q4; *3*. Kt—QB3, B—Kt5; *4*. B—Q2, P×P; *5*. Q—Kt4, Kt—KB3; *6*. Q×KtP, R—Kt1; *7*. Q—R6, Q×P; *8*. O—O—O, Kt—Kt5; *9*. Q—R4, Q×P; *10*. Q—Q8 ch, resigns, because of *10*. .... K×Q; *11*. B—Kt5 db ch, K—K1; *12*. R—Q8 mate.

Still prettier, but with the same idea, is the following famous off-hand game played in Vienna 1908. White Réti, Black Dr Tartakower.   *1*. P—K4,   P—QB3;   *2*. P—Q4,   P—Q4; *3*. Kt—QB3, P×P; *4*. Kt×P, Kt—B3; *5*. Q—Q3, P—K4; *6*. P×P, Q—R4 ch; *7*. B—Q2, Q×KP; *8*. O—O—O, Kt × Kt; *9*. Q—Q8 ch, K × Q; *10*. B—Kt5 db ch, K—B2; *11*. B—Q8 mate.

Discovered check can win material in a variety of ways. In Diagram 81 play continued *30*. P×P, R×R; *31*. R × R, resigns. For if *31*. .... Kt×P; *32* P—B6 dis ch wins the exchange.

So great is the power of this weapon that even a Queen can be surrendered to obtain a series of discovered checks (Diagram 82).

Black (Horowitz)

81

White (Fine) to play
New York, 1951

Black (Em. Lasker)

White (Torre) to play
Moscow, 1925

White played *25.* B – B6, Q × Q; *26.* R × P ch, K – R1; *27.* R × P dis ch, K – Kt1; *28.* R – Kt7 ch, K – R1; *29.* R × B dis ch, K – Kt1; *30.* R – Kt7 ch, K – R1; *31.* R – Kt5 dis ch, K – R2; *32.* R × Q, K – Kt3; *33.* R – R3, K × B; *34.* R × P ch, and won.

In the next example discovered check alone is not enough, but wins in conjunction with the strength of the queening Pawn (Diagram 83) by *1.* .... Q – K8 ch; *2.* R × Q, P – B7 dis ch; *3.* Q × B, P × R=Q ch; *4.* K – Kt2, Q × R ch.

Black (Rubinstein) to play

White (Salwe)
Lodz, 1908

Black (Sir George Thomas)

White (Dr Ed. Lasker) to play
London, 1913

Diagram 84 again demonstrates a Queen sacrifice solely to gain the all-important discovered and double check. Now came *1.* Q × P ch, K × Q; *2.* Kt × B db ch, K – R3; *3.* Kt(K5) – Kt4 ch, K – Kt4; *4.* P – R4 ch, K – B5; *5.* P – Kt3 ch, K – B6; *6.* B – K2 ch, K – Kt7; *7.* R – R2 ch, K – Kt8; *8.* O – O – O mate.

Note that Castles can also be a deadly blow as a combination. It is rare that one administers mate with it as above, but material can be won by such typical moves as in Diagram 85 where by

85

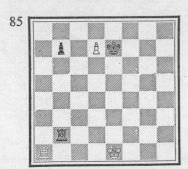

White to play and win
79

1. O − O − O, White either wins the Rook or forces his Pawn on to Queen.

Discovered check can also give rise to a special and most pleasing type of mate by which the King is smothered by its own pieces – hence it is called 'smothered mate'. Diagram 86 gives

86

White to play

87 Black (B. H. Wood)

White (Morry) to play
Birmingham, 1950

the basic type. White plays *1.* Q−Q5 ch, K−R1; *2.* Kt−B7 ch, K−Kt1; *3.* Kt−R6 db ch, K−R1; *4.* Q−Kt8 ch, R×Q; *5.* Kt−B7 mate.

It is well to bear this manœuvre (or its threat) in mind since though the Philidor mate (so called after the greatest chess-player of the eighteenth century, André Danican Philidor) is hundreds of years old it still occurs frequently as, for example, in Diagram 87 where White continues *28.* K−B1, R−Q7; *29.* K−K1, Q−R5; (hoping for *30.* K×R, Q×P ch; when he can still struggle on for some moves) but *30.* Q−Kt3 ch, resigns because of *30.* .... K−R1; *31.* Kt−B7 ch, K−Kt1; *32.* Kt−R6 db ch, K−R1; *33.* Q−Kt8 ch, R×Q; *34.* Kt−B7 mate.

THE BACK RANK

Many combinations are based on a threat of mate on the back rank which can prove most profitable for the attacker and exasperating for the defendant. An elementary example is shown in Diagram 88. If Black is so rash as to capture the Pawn on R2 White mates by R – K8.

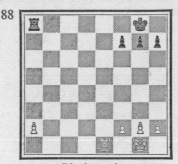

Black to play

Black (Radalescu)

White (Golombek) to play
Bucarest, 1953

In such positions and in those where the files are open so that the Rooks can range up and down the board at will it is essential to give the King a loophole for escape. In Diagram 89 White utilized his better development and Black's lack of a loophole to win a Pawn and eventually the game by *18. Kt × P*, since Black was unable to reply *18. .... R × Kt; 19. B × R, Kt × B;* because of *20. R — Q8 ch,* followed by mate.

Both sides are in peril on the back rank in Diagram 90. If White now plays *21. R × P?* then *21. .... R × R ch; 22. B × R, R — Q8* mate. But White can exploit his opponent's back rank weakness by *21. R — B7!* and after *21. .... K — B1; 22. R × R*

Black (Aitken)

90

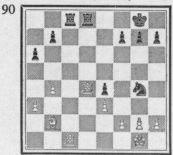

White (Golombek) to play
Hastings, 1947

Black (Euwe)

91

White (Reshevsky) to play
New York, 1951

ch, R × R; *23.* B — Q4, Kt — K4; *24.* R × P, he won a Pawn and the game.

White's failure to realize his weakness on the back rank caused him to commit a blunder in Diagram 91. Instead of playing *1.* Kt × Kt, followed by P — KR3 with rather the better game, he went *1.* Q — Q7, and after *1.* .... R — Q1! White had to lose his Queen or be mated.

In Diagram 92 White utilized the back rank to force a mating

92   Black (Lelichuk)   93   Black (Stoltz)

White (Ezersky) to play   White (Sliwa) to play
U.S.S.R., 1950   Bucarest, 1953

attack on another point by *16.* Q — R4, and whatever reply Black makes he cannot escape mate.

The next example, Diagram 93, is a pretty fantasia on the theme of the back rank which goes *33.* Q × B!, P × Q; *34.* P — Kt7, Q — Q1; *35.* P — Kt8 = Q, R — Q8 ch; *36.* R × R, Q × Q; *37.* Kt — Kt7!, P — QB4; *38.* R — Q8 ch, Q × R; *39.* Kt × Q, K — B1; *40.* K — B1, K — K1; *41.* Kt — Kt7, resigns.

Sometimes the loophole a player has devised is more seeming than real. In Diagram 94 White would be quite all right if, for instance, he had the Pawn structure, Pawns on KB2, KKt3, and KR2. As it is he loses at once after *19.* .... B — Q3!, since loss of the Queen or mate is inevitable.

Black (Morel) to play

White (Johner)
Neuenburg, 1952

Perhaps the most ingenious and beautiful series of combinations based on the back rank mate occurred in the position in Diagram 95. White played *18*. Q—KKt4!, Q—Kt4; *19*. Q—QB4! (not *19*. P—QR4, Q×R!; *20*. R×Q, R—B8 ch; and Black mates) *19*. .... Q—Q2; *20*. Q—B7!, Q—Kt4; *21*. P—QR4, Q×RP;

Black (Torre)

White (Adams) to play
New Orleans, 1920

22. R — K4, Q — Kt4; *23.* Q × KtP!, resigns since he cannot answer all the threats.

STALEMATE POSSIBILITIES

Usually stalemate occurs in the end-game phase when there is little material left on either side; but sometimes it appears out of the blue in the middle game. The time to be wary is when one side is at his last gasp and when the other has overwhelming material or positional superiority. Black must have felt the game was all over in Diagram 96 when he now played *37.* .... R × B; as

96 Black (Tylor) to play

White (Fairhurst)
Ramsgate, 1929

97 Black (Lange)

White (Danielsson) to play
Helsinki, 1952

indeed it was, for White replied *38.* R(B1) — B7 ch, and after *38.* .... R × R; *39.* R × R ch, K × R; stalemate. Or if *39.* .... K — R3; *40.* R × P ch, K × R; stalemate.

Still more marked is the next example (Diagram 97) where White carelessly played *50.* Q — Q5? (correct was *50.* Q — R5, followed by Q — K5) allowing a forced stalemate by *50.* .... R × P ch; *51.* K — B1, Q — R8 ch; *52.* K — K2, R — K6 ch; *53.* K × R, Q — K8 ch; *54.* K — B3, Q — K6 ch; *55.* P × Q.

Use of the threat of stalemate to restore equality is shown in

Black (Cholmov) to play

White (Keres)
Moscow, 1948

Diagram 98 where Black played *46.* .... Q–Kt5 ch!
47. K–R2, Q–R4 ch; *48.* K–Kt2, Q–Kt5 ch; *49.* K–B1,
Q × RP; and the game was agreed a draw after another 13 moves.

CHAPTER 5

THE MIDDLE GAME:
COMBINATION PLAY AND ATTACK

In Chapter 3 the vital necessity of development was emphasized and this need becomes still more obvious when we try to combine pieces in an attack. *It is of no use whatsoever to start combining until you have developed your pieces.* Many a game has been lost through the forgetting or ignorance of this simple rule and one often sees a player in difficulties through indulgence in Pawn moves in the opening at the expense of piece development.

A succinct illustration: White Gibaud, Black Lazard, Paris, 1924: *1.* P—Q4, Kt—KB3; *2.* Kt—Q2, P—K4; *3.* P×P, Kt—Kt5; *4.* P—KR3? (one Pawn move too many; simply *4.* KKt—B3, was correct) *4.* .... Kt—K6! White resigns.

Equally bad is the moving of the same piece more than once early on in the game. This led to a quick loss in the following game from the International Team Tournament at Helsinki, 1952. White Golombek (Gt Britain), Black Planas (Cuba): *1.* P—QB4, P—K4; *2.* Kt—QB3, Kt—QB3; *3.* P—KKt3, P—QKt3; *4.* B—Kt2, B—Kt2; *5.* Kt—R3, Kt—R4? (serious loss of time; he should play *5.* .... Kt—B3) *6.* B×B, Kt×B; *7.* P—B4, P×P; *8.* Kt×P, Kt—B3; *9.* P—K4, P—KR3; (another sin against the rules of development) *10.* O—O, B—K2; *11.* Q—B3 (threatening to win a piece by *12.* P—K5, and so forcing Black to make the ensuing awkward move) *11.* .... Q—Kt1; *12.* KKt—Q5, Kt—Q1; (note that Black is compelled to continue with the weakening policy of moving the same piece: he must guard KB2 against White's threat of P—K5) *13.* Kt×B, K×Kt; *14.* P—K5, Kt—K1; (if *14.* .... Kt—R2; *15.* Kt—Q5 ch, K—K1; *16.* Kt×P ch); *15.* P—Q4, K—B1; *16.* B—K3, K—Kt1; *17.* Kt—Q5 (threatening *18.* Q—B5, followed by Kt—K7 ch and Kt—Kt6 ch) *17.* .... P—Kt3; *18.* Q—Kt4,

K—Kt2; (or *18*. .... Kt—K3; *19*. Kt—K7 ch, K—Kt2; *20*. Kt—B5 ch, K—R2; *21*. Kt×P) *19*. Q×P, Q—B1; (if *19*. P—B3; *20*. P—K6, P×Kt; *21*. R×P ch, Kt×R; *22*. Q×Kt mate) *20*. P—K6, Q×Q; *21*. P×Q, Kt—Q3; *22*. Kt×BP, R—QKt1; *23*. B—B4, resigns. For if *23*. .... Kt×P; *24*. Kt—K8 ch, or if *23*. .... Kt(Q1)—Kt2; *24*. B—K5 ch.

PREMATURE QUEEN DEVELOPMENT

Do not rush out your Queen early in the game. The minor pieces (Kt and B) should be developed first; for you may incur loss of time through having to retreat the Queen when attacked by pieces of lesser value, or you may even lose the Queen through getting it surrounded by enemy pieces.

How it loses time is shown by an indifferent defence known as the Centre Counter Defence: *1*. P—K4, P—Q4; *2*. P×P, Q×P; *3*. Kt—QB3, and now the Queen must move again. In this defence Black is always behindhand in development, but worse still can befall the side that prematurely brings out the Queen. The following three brevities illustrate this:

From a tournament played at Bad Lausich in 1951, White Fetzer, Black Schmidt: *1*. P—K4, P—QB4; *2*. Kt—KB3, Kt—QB3; *3*. P—B3, P—Q3; *4*. P—Q4, P×P; *5*. P×P, Kt—B3; *6*. Kt—B3, P—K3; *7*. B—KKt5, B—K2; *8*. B—Q3, Q—Kt3? (O—O should be played) *9*. Kt—QR4, Q—Kt5 ch (Black should acknowledge the error and play Q—Q1) *10*. B—Q2, resigns as the Queen is lost!

The above occurred between two weak players but even great masters may succumb. See the following from the great international tournament at Moscow in 1935. White Botvinnik, Black Spielmann: *1*. P—QB4, P—QB3; *2*. P—K4, P—Q4; *3*. KP×P, P×P; *4*. P—Q4, Kt—KB3; *5*. Kt—QB3, Kt—B3; *6*. B—Kt5, Q—Kt3? (correct is P—K3) *7*. P×P, Q×KtP; *8*. R—B1, QKt—Kt5; *9*. Kt—R4, Q×RP; *10*. B—QB4, B—Kt5; *11*. Kt—KB3, B×Kt; *12*. P×B, resigns. For if he wishes to save his Queen he must give up a piece by *12*. .... Q—R6; *13*. R—B3, Kt—B7 ch.

In the next example, from the International Team Tournament at Dubrovnik 1950, it is White who gets into trouble with his Queen. White Castaldi, Black Reshevsky: *1.* Kt — KB3, P — Q4; *2.* P — KKt3, Kt — KB3; *3.* B — Kt2, P — KKt3; *4.* O — O, B — Kt2; *5.* P — B4, P — Q5; *6.* P — K3, P — B4; *7.* P × P, P × P; *8.* P — Q3, Kt — B3; *9.* Q — R4? (so bad is this premature sortie with the Queen that in only four more moves White can resign; instead he should play *9.* R — K1, and if *9.* .... O — O; *10.* B — B4) *9.* .... O — O; *10.* P — QKt4, Kt — Q2; *11.* QKt — Q2, P — QR4; *12.* B — R3, P × P; *13.* Q × R, Kt — Kt3; White resigns – the Queen is lost.

The conclusion to draw from all this is that if weak player and master alike get into trouble from premature Q development then no matter what your strength is as a player you should shun this practice like the plague.

THE KING IN THE CENTRE

Whilst most pieces exert their greatest influence in central positions the King (until and except the end game) is too vulnerable a piece for the hurly-burly of central operations and should be tucked away in the flank as soon as possible. Many a game

Black (Wade) to play

99

White (Delfin)
Glasgow, 1953

has been lost through leaving the King too long in the middle. In Diagram 99 White has put off castling far too long and now Black plays *19. .... Kt—Q5! 20. Q—Q1* (if *20. P×Kt, P×P; 21. B×P, B×B;* with great advantage to Black) *20. .... Q—K2;* (threat Kt×P ch) *21. Q—R4, P—K5; 22. P—B4,* (if *22. P×Kt, P×P) 22. .... Kt×B; 23. K×Kt, B×B; 24. P×B, R—Q6; 25. KR—Q1, Q—B4; 26. K—B1, Q×KP;* and Black won.

In Diagram 100, Black, having neglected to castle when he

100

White (Spielmann) to play
7th match-game, Rogaska–Slatina, 1931

had the opportunity, finds his King drawn into a most vulnerable position by *11. Kt×KBP!, K×Kt; 12. Q—B3, P—KKt3; 13. Kt×Kt, B×P ch; 14. K×B, Q—R5 ch; 15. K—Kt1, Q×Kt; 16. Q—Kt3, KR—K1; 17. B—Q2, Q—B7; 18. B—B3, Kt—Q4; 19. KR—B1, Q—K5; 20. B—Q2,* (threatening to win the Queen by P—B3) *20. .... P—KKt4; 21. P—B3, Q—R5; 22. Q×Q, P×Q; 23. P—K4, B—Kt3; 24. P×Kt, KP×P; 25. B—B1,* resigns.

A common cause for this slowness to castle is the ambition to attack the enemy King before one's own is in safety. In Diagram 101 Black should castle, instead of which he rashly plays *11. ....*

Black (Lipnitsky) to play

101

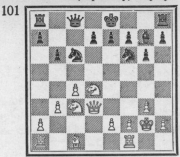

White (Nej)
Semi-final, U.S.S.R. Championship, 1951

P—KR4?; *12.* B—Kt2, P—R5; *13.* Kt—B3, P×P; *14.* RP×P,
Kt—QKt5; *15.* Q—Q2, P—Q4?; (with the King still in the
centre he should not open up his position; instead *15.* ....
P—Q3 should be played) *16.* R—R1, R×R; *17.* R×R, P×P;
18. P—R3, Kt—R3; *19.* Kt—Q5, Q—B3; *20.* P×P, Kt—B2;
21. B—K5, Kt(B2)×Kt; *22.* P×Kt, Q—B4; *23.* R—QB1,
Q×RP; *24.* P—Q6, P×P; *25.* B×P, Q—R5; *26.* R—B7,
Q—Kt6; *27.* R—K7 ch, K—Q1; *28.* Kt—K5, (threatening mate
by *29.* Kt—B6 ch, K—B1; *30.* R—B7) *28.* .... Q—Q4 ch;
29. P—K4!, resigns; for if *29.* .... Q×Q; *30.* Kt—B6 ch
followed by mate. Or if *29.* .... Q×P ch; *30.* P—B3, Q—Q4;
31. Kt×P ch, K—B1; *32.* Q—B2 ch, etc.

INITIAL WEAKNESSES

If you look at the board with the pieces unmoved you will
find that the one point round the King that is the least guarded is
KB2. This is undoubtedly the most vulnerable point on the
board until a player gets castled and many combinations are
based on this danger point.

How quickly KB2 can be undermined appears in the following
game from the Prague International Team Tournament, 1931.

White Horowitz (U.S.A.), Black Gudju (Rumania): *1.* P—K4, P—QB3; *2.* P—Q4, P—Q4; *3.* Kt—QB3, P×P; *4.* Kt×P, B—B4; *5.* Kt—Kt3, B—Kt3; *6.* P—KR4, P—KR3; *7.* Kt—B3, P—K3?; (better *7.* .... Kt—Q2); *8.* Kt—K5, B—R2; *9.* B—QB4, Kt—Q2; *10.* Q—K2, KKt—B3?; (Kt×Kt must be played) *11.* Kt×KBP!, B—Kt5 ch; (if *11.* .... K×Kt; *12.* Q×P ch, K—Kt3; *13.* P—R5 mate) *12.* P—B3, resigns.

The presence of a Kt on K5 should always sound a warning note for the defending player. The above and the following game emphasize this. White Karaklaic, Black Matanovic, Yugoslavia, 1948: *1.* P—K4, P—K3; *2.* P—Q4, P—Q4; *3.* Kt—QB3, P×P; *4.* Kt×P, Kt—Q2; *5.* B—Q3, KKt—B3; *6.* Q—K2, P—QKt3; *7.* Kt—KB3, B—Kt2; *8.* Kt—K5, B—K2?; (correct was *8.* .... QKt×Kt;) *9.* Kt×P, K×Kt; *10.* Kt—Kt5 ch, K—K1; *11.* Kt×KP, Q—B1; *12.* B—KB4, P—B4; *13.* Kt×P ch, K—B2; *14.* Q—K6 ch, K—B1; *15.* Kt—B5, Kt—Q4; *16.* Kt—Q6! resigns as if *16.* .... B×Kt; *17.* B—R6 mate.

Black (Lehtonen) to play

102

White (Kulmala)
Helsinki, 1938

Too many Pawn moves in front of the King may be responsible for disaster on KB2. In Diagram 102 Black played the startling *8.* .... Q—R5 ch! *9.* Kt×Q, B—B7 ch; *10.* K—K2, Kt—Q5 ch; *11.* K—Q3, Kt—B4 mate.

Even after castling a player may find his KB2 a weak point, especially if his KR has been exchanged or lured away from KB1. In Diagram 103 White wins by *21.* Kt × P!, K × Kt;

Black (Gonsior)

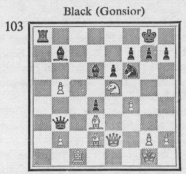

103

White (Vyslouzil) to play
Semi-final Czechoslovak Championship, 1952

22. B−B4, Q × P(Kt7); *23.* Q × P ch, K−Kt3; *24.* P−B5 ch, K−R4; *25.* B−K2 ch, K−R5; (or *25.* .... Kt−Kt5; *26.* B × Kt ch, K × B; *27.* P−R3 ch, K−R5; *28.* Q−K1 ch, B−Kt6; *29.* Q−K7 ch, P−Kt4; *30.* Q × P mate) *26.* Q × B, resigns as he is mated in a few moves.

Another weak initial point is QB2, though here it is the Queen rather than the King that is in danger. Take the following brevity played in a match between Vienna and Amsterdam in 1950. White Dr Heen, Black Telleman: *1.* P−K4, Kt−KB3; *2.* Kt−QB3, P−Q4; *3.* P × P, Kt × P; *4.* P−Q4, B−B4; *5.* KKt−K2? (better is *5.* B−QB4,) *5.* .... Kt−Kt5; *6.* B−K3, B × P; White resigns as he must lose his Queen.

ATTACKS ON (AND DEFENCE OF) THE CASTLED KING

By far the commonest type of combinative attack is that on the castled King. In this it is essential for the attacking side *to have all* (*or as many as possible*) *of his pieces to join in the assault.* An attack by a few pieces against an enemy prepared to repulse it with a large number merely results in loss of time or material.

The defender must bear two things in mind.

(1) *A minor piece (Kt or B) must be handy on the K side to protect the King.*

(2) *The best Pawn protection of a King is an unmoved Pawn position.* The next best is a fianchettoed Bishop structure (i.e. B on KKt2 and Pawns on KR2, KKt3, and KB2). But in this last formation there exists the danger that one's opponent may succeed in exchanging off Bishops and leaving you with serious weaknesses on KR3 and KB3.

The basic attacking positions on the point KR2 are shown in Diagrams 104 and 105; those for KKt2 on Diagrams 106 and 107, and that for KB2 on Diagram 108.

The most sensitive point of all is KR2 and it is here that the defence most often gives way. In Diagram 109 the weakness is revealed by one significant blow. Black has just played 29. .... R × P(KB5); hoping for *30*. R × R, |P – Kt3; when he has emerged from his trouble but instead White replied *30*. R – R8, whereupon Black resigned since KR2 was not to be defended.

Unless the defender has a minor piece on the King side he may often find that the attack will break through by means of a

104   105

Attack on KR2   Attack on KR2

106

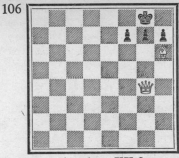

Attack on KKt2

107

Attack on KKt2

108

Attack on KB2

Black (Ragosin)

White (Tchekhover) to play
Moscow, 1936 (Young Masters' Tournament)

White to play

sacrifice on KR2. The typical position is Diagram 110 where
White plays *1.* B × P ch, K × B; *2.* Kt—Kt5 ch, and now if
2. .... K—Kt3; *3.* Q—Kt4, followed by a deadly discovered
check with the Kt; or if *2.* .... K—Kt1; *3.* Q—R5, R—K1;
4. Q × P ch, K—R1; *5.* Q—R5 ch, K—Kt1; *6.* Q—R7 ch,
K—B1; *7.* Q—R8 ch, K—K2; *8.* Q × P mate. The Belgian
master, E. Colle, specialized in attacks of this kind and with them

achieved many brilliant finishes. In Diagram 111 even though
Black had a minor piece ready to go to the defence of his King
Colle broke through with a cascade of brilliancies: *12.* B×P ch,
K×B; *13.* Kt−Kt5 ch, K−Kt3; *14.* P−KR4, (threatening
15. P−R5 ch, K−B3; *16.* Q−B3 ch) *14.* .... R−R1;
15. R×P ch!, Kt−B3; *16.* P−R5 ch, K−R3; (if *16.* ....
R×P; *17.* Q−Q3 ch, K−R3; *18.* Kt×P mate) *17.* R×B,
Q−R4; *18.* Kt×P db ch, K−R2; *19.* Kt−Kt5 ch, K−Kt1;
20. Q−Kt3 ch, resigns.

This Bishop sacrifice is also effective when the defence has
already allowed his K side to become rather ragged: as in
Diagram 112 where White played *16.* B×P ch, K×B; *17.* Kt−

111   Black (O'Hanlon)   112   Black (Kotov)

White (Colle) to play   White (Kottnauer) to play
Nice, 1930   Match Prague–Moscow, 1946

Kt5 ch, K−Kt3; *18.* Q−Kt4, P−B4; *19.* Q−Kt3, K−B3;
20. B−B4, K−K2; *21.* QR−B1, (threatening *22.* B−B7,
Q−B3; *23.* P−Kt4) *21.* .... R−R2; *22.* KR−K1, B−Q2;
23. P−Kt4, Kt−R3; *24.* Kt×P, B×Kt; *25.* Q×B ch, R−B2;
26. B−Kt5 ch, K−Q2; *27.* Q−R8, Q−Kt1; *28.* Q×P ch,
resigns.

The defender may think he has his KR2 adequately protected
only to succumb to a discovered attack on the protection itself.
By an odd chance it is Kotov again who is the sufferer in an

Black (Kotov) to play

113

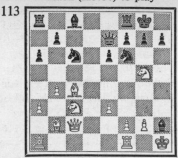

White (Szabo)
Groningen, 1946

example of this in Diagram 113. Instead of *15. .... B − K4;* which would have held the position, he committed the instructive blunder of *15. .... P − R3;* when came *16. Kt − Q5, P × Kt (Q4); 17. B × Kt, B − B4; 18. Q × B, P − KKt3;* and now White's simplest and quickest win is by *19. B × Q, P × Q; 20. B × R,* though he actually played *19. Q × P ch,* and still won in another ten moves.

Black (Del Vecchio)

114

White (Porreca) to play
Ferrara, 1952

The discovered attack is just as effective when concentrated on KKt2. In Diagram 114 Black would be quite all right if he had a minor piece on the K side – say a Bishop on KB3; but as it is White wins by *14.* R × Kt, Q × R; *15.* Kt × P, Q – B1; *16.* B × B, Q × B; *17.* Kt – Kt6, resigns; because of *17.* .... B – B3; *18.* Kt – K7 ch, K – R1; *19.* Q × B, P × Q; *20.* B × P mate.

The necessity for having a minor piece on the K side cannot be over-emphasized. In Diagram 115 if Black had a Kt on KB1

115   Black (Ivanov)

White (Milev) to play
Bulgaria, 1952

116   Black (Weil)

White (Sir George Thomas)
to play
Klosterneuburg, 1934

he would be safe. The Rook is worse than useless and one should beware of positions with King on R1 and Rook on KKt1. The latter piece, as often as not, merely chokes up Black's King's way to safety. Here after *1.* R × P ch, Black resigned because of *1.* .... K × R; *2.* Q – R3 ch, K – Kt2; *3.* B – R6 ch, and now if (*a*) *3.* .... K – B2; *4.* Q – K6 mate, or if (*b*) *3.* .... K – R2 (R1); *4.* B – B8 mate.

What happens when you move Pawns in front of your King is shown in Diagram 116. White played *18.* P – KR3, and his K side was then broken up by *18.* .... B × RP; *19.* P × B, Q × P; *20.* Kt – R2, B – K4; *21.* P – B3, B × Kt ch; *22.* Q × B,

Black (Hirschbein)

White (Rubinstein) to play
Lodz, 1927

R — Kt3 ch; White resigns. Again, in Diagram 117, the advance of a Pawn in front of the King results in disaster. White finished off the game beautifully by *21.* R × Kt!, B × R; *22.* Kt — B6 ch, K — B1; *23.* Kt — Q5!, resigns.

Pawns advanced in front of the King provide an easy target for attack and must be avoided. In Diagram 118 White breaks

Black (Kahn)

White (Richter) to play
Prague International Team Tournament, 1931

down the feeble barrier made by the advanced K-side Pawns in half a dozen moves. *19.* P—KR4, Kt—Kt3; (if *19.* .... P×P; *20.* Q×P, and White will continue the attack by P—KB4—B5) *20.* P×P, P×P; *21.* Q×P, Q—K3; *22.* Kt—R5 ch, K—B1; *23.* R—Q1, B—Q2; *24.* Kt—B6, B—K1; *25.* Q—R6 ch, K—K2; (or *25.* .... R×Q; *26.* B×R ch, K—K2; *27.* Kt—Kt8 mate) *26.* Kt—Kt8 ch, resigns because of *26.* .... R×Kt; *27.* B—Kt5 ch, P—B3; *28.* P×P ch, etc.

A similar process, but one even more brilliant and convincing, is shown in Diagram 119. The game continued *20.* P—KB4!

Black (Lebedew)

119

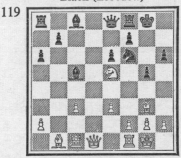

White (Mikenas) to play
Gruzinske, 1941

B×P ch; *21.* K—R1, B×R; *22.* P×P, B×P; *23.* R×Kt, K—Kt2 (if *23.* .... B×R; *24.* Q—Q3, forces mate) *24.* Q—Q3, P—KR4; (again mate comes after *24.* .... K×R; *25.* Kt—Kt4 ch) *25.* P—KR4, K×R; *26.* Kt—Kt4 ch, P×Kt; *27.* B—K5 ch, K×B; *28.* Q—Q4 mate.

STRIPPING THE K SIDE

When the defence has not weakened itself by Pawn moves it becomes necessary to break through by forceful sacrifice, or sacrifices. The pattern to be observed here is the sacrifice of minor pieces in order to pave the way for the major ones (the Rooks and Queens). One of the most dramatic combinations of this type is the double Bishop sacrifice as seen in Diagram 120.

Black (Bauer)

120

White (Em. Lasker) to play
Amsterdam, 1889

Lasker played *14*. Kt−R5, Kt×Kt; *15*. B×P ch, K×B; *16*. Q×Kt ch, K−Kt1; *17*. B×P!, K×B; *18*. Q−Kt4 ch, K−R2; *19*. R−B3, P−K4; *20*. R−R3 ch, Q−R3; *21*. R× Q ch, K×R; *22*. Q−Q7, B−KB3; *23*. Q×B, K−Kt2; *24*. R− ·KB1, QR−Kt1; *25*. Q−Q7, KR−Q1; *26*. Q−Kt4 ch, K−B1; *27*. P×P, B−Kt2; (or *27*. .... B×P; *28*. Q−B5, winning the Bishop) *28*. P−K6, R−Kt2; *29*. Q−Kt6, P−B3; *30*. R×P ch, B×R; *31*. Q×B ch, K−K1; *32*. Q−R8 ch, K−K2; *33*. Q−Kt7 ch, resigns.

A modern variation on the same theme is shown in Diagram 121. White played *21*. B×P ch, K×B; *22*. Q−R5 ch, K−Kt1; *23*. B×P, K×B; *24*. R−R3, Q−B2; (so that if *25*. R−Kt3 ch, Q×R) *25*. R−Q7!, B−Q3; (or *25*. .... Q×R; *26*. R−Kt3 ch, K−B3; *27*. Q−Kt5 mate) *26*. Q−Kt5 ch, K−R2; *27*. R×Q, B×R; *28*. Q−K7, QR−B1; *29*. R−KB3, P−B4; *30*. Q− R4 ch, K−Kt2; *31*. Q−Kt5 ch, K−R1; *32*. R−B6, B−K5; *33*. R−R6 ch, B−R2; *34*. Q−R5, resigns.

Black (Dr Cornforth)

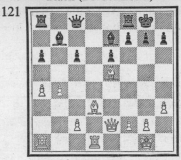

White (König) to play
National Club Championship, London, 1952

Elimination of the KKtP alone will frequently allow the attacker to force through his assault with a Rook or Queen along the KKt file. In Diagram 122 the sacrifices achieve this with brilliant suddenness. *22.* B × P, P × B; *23.* R × P ch! (even a major piece is sacrificed in the interests of stripping the K side) *23.* .... K × R; *24.* Q − B6 ch, K − Kt1; *25.* R − Kt1 ch,

Black (Mieses)

White (Bogoljubow) to play
Baden-Baden, 1925

Q—Kt5; *26.* R×Q ch, P×R; *27.* P—B5, R(Q1)—QB1; *28.* P—K6, B—B3; *29.* Q—B7 ch, K—R1; *30.* P—B6, R—KKt1; *31.* Q—B7, QR—B1; *32.* Q—K5, P—Q5 dis ch; *33.* K—Kt1, resigns.

In Diagram 123 the K side is stripped to allow the Queen and

123 Black (Rethy) to play

White (Danielsson)
International Team Tournament,
Warsaw, 1935

124 Black (Norman-Hansen)

White (Golombek) to play
Margate, 1937

Bishop to work together and form a mating net by *24.* .... Kt×P! *25.* R—K3, (if *25.* K×Kt, B—B6 ch; *26.* K—Kt1, Q—R6) *25.* .... Q—R6; *26.* Kt—B1, B—B6; *27.* R×B, P×R; *28.* Kt—K3, Kt×P; White resigns.

Under threat of mate Black is forced to advance his K-side Pawns and allow the stripping process in Diagram 124. White played *19.* Q—R5, (threatening *20.* Kt—B6 ch, P×Kt; *21.* P×P, Queen moves; *22.* Q—Kt5 ch, followed by mate) *19.* .... P—KB4; *20.* P×P *e.p.*, P×P; *21.* Kt×P ch, K—R1; (if *21.* .... R×Kt; *22.* Q—Kt5 ch, K—B2; *23.* R×R ch, Q×R; *24.* R—B1) *22.* Q—K5, Q—Kt2; *23.* R—B4, P—B4; *24.* R(B1)—B1, P×P; *25.* Kt—R5, resigns.

Breaking down the K side when the enemy Pawn is on KKt3 can be accomplished by advancing one's own RP to R5, or else a piece sacrifice can undermine the base as in Diagram 125. White played 23. Kt×RP, K×Kt; 24. R−R5 ch, K−Kt2; 25. Q−R4!, P×R; 26. Q−Kt5 ch, K−R2; 27. Q×P ch, K−Kt2; 28. Q−Kt5 ch, K−R1; 29. R−K4, resigns. For if 29. ....P−B3; 30. Q−R6 ch, Q−R2; 31. Q×R ch, and mates next move.

It is the Kt and B in unison that form the mating attack in the next example (Diagram 126) and so strip the King bare. Black

125   Black (Canal)   126   Black (Dvorak) to play

White (Christoffel) to play   White (Mudra)
Zurich, 1952   Marianske–Lanze, 1951

continued 18. .... Kt(B3)−Q5; 19. P×Kt, Kt×P; 20. Q−K3, P−KB5; 21. P×P, P×P; 22. Kt×P, R×Kt; 23. B−Kt2, (if 23. Q×R, Kt−K7 mate) 23. .... B×B; 24. K×B, Q−Q4 ch; 25. P−B3, R×P; White resigns.

DIVERSIONARY AND ELIMINATORY SACRIFICES

In order to force through one's attack against the King it is often necessary to remove the protection afforded to the said King by one of its guarding pieces. To achieve this a sacrifice is made either to divert the piece away from the King or else to eliminate it. Sometimes one can eliminate one piece and divert another – as

Black (Pytlakowski)

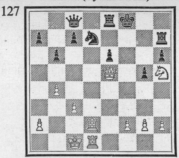

White (Balanel) to play
Marianske–Lazne, 1951

in Diagram 127 where White won by *1*. R × Kt, (elimination)
1. .... R × R; (the Rook is diverted from guarding the King)
2. Q – R8 ch, K – K2; *3*. Q – B6 mate.

It is no accident that the Knight is the piece that requires
eliminating. For it is the piece that gives the King the best
protection and it is therefore the piece that must be destroyed
before an attack can succeed. In Diagram 128 it is overworked

Black (Heidenfeld)

White (Toran) to play
Beverwijk, 1953

and the final sacrifice comes as a merciful release. White played *1*. B × P ch, when Black resigned because of *1*. .... Kt × B; *2*. Q−Kt5 ch, K−B1; (or *2*. .... K−R1; *3*. Q−B6 mate) *3*. Q × Kt ch, K−K2; *4*. Q−Kt5 ch, K−B1; *5*. Q−B6 ch and mate next move.

How important the Knight is appears in Diagram 129

Black (Averbach)

129

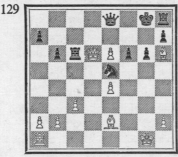

White (Gusev) to play
Moscow, 1946

where White, owing to the strength of his passed Pawn on K6 can give up his Queen to suppress the enemy piece. White played *24*. Q × Kt!, P × Q; *25*. R − KB1, (threatening B − QKt5) *25*. .... R − B1; (if *25*. .... R × P; *26*. B − QB4, or if *25*. .... R − B2; *26*. B − QKt5, and White wins) *26*. B − Q1, R − B5; (if *26*. .... Q × P; *27*. B − Kt3, wins) *27*. B − Kt3, P − QKt4; *28*. B × R, P × B; *29*. P − Kt3, P − R4; *30*. P × P, Q − K2; *31*. K − Kt2, (more precise is *31*. K − R1, when the King would not be exposed to checks) *31*. .... Q − R6; *32*. R − B2, (White is in time trouble and wastes moves hereabouts. A quicker win was *32*. R − B7, Q − Kt7 ch; *33*. K − Kt3, Q × BP ch; *34*. K − Kt4, Q − R6; *35*. P − B5!, Q × BP; *36*. R − Kt7 ch, K − B1; *37*. R − QB7 dis ch, etc.) *32*. .... Q − K2; *33*. R − B1, P − Kt4; *34*. R − B5, P − Kt5; (now the Black Queen must guard not only KB1 but KKt4 and can move only from Q1 to K2 and back.

So he must helplessly watch the QBP proceed to queen) *35*. P—B5, Q—Q1; *36*. P—B6, Q—K2; *37*. P—B7, resigns.

Now an example where it is merely necessary to eliminate a Pawn so as to administer the *coup de grâce* (Diagram 130),

130 Black (L. Schmid) to play   131 Black (Rebizzo) to play

White (Hoffman)
Match game, 1946

White (Nadjorf)
Buenos Aires, 1951

Black forces mate by *34*. .... R × RP ch; *35*. K × R, R—R5 ch; *36*. K—Kt3, Kt—R4.

THE INTERVENTION

The best way of meeting force is by counter-force; so, since the strongest moves always involve a check, the ideal way to deal with a check is by a check in return. See Diagram 131 where Black's *37*. .... Q—K4 ch was met by *38*. R—Kt3 ch, and Black resigned.

EXCHANGE COMBINATIONS

One can often combine to force a number of exchanges either in order to gain material or else to bring about a won ending. The exchanges that are made in Diagram 132 yield Black a piece

Black (Alexander) to play

132

White (Dr Fazekas)
Ilford, 1953

after *24.* .... R(K1) × B; *25.* R × B ch, (if *25.* Kt × R, R − B8 ch)
25. .... Q × R; *26.* Q × R, R × Kt.

In Diagram 133 White uses this idea to win a Pawn and

Black (Euwe) to play

133

White (Bouwmeester)
Dutch Championship, 1952

procure a won end game. Note that the idea of progress by
exchange continues right to the very end. Black played *33.* ....
P−QKt4; (if *33.* .... P−Q6; *34.* R−K8, R × R; *35.* Q × R,

109

and wins) and then came *34.* Q × R !, R × Q; *35.* R − K8 ch, R − B1; *36.* R × Q, B × R; *37.* B × QP, B − Q2; *38.* B − K5, R − B2; *39.* R − Q1; K − Kt1; *40.* B − Kt4, resigns as a piece is lost.

Exchanges solely to obtain a superior ending without thought of immediate gain in material occur in Diagram 134. This

134   Black (Vidmar)

White (Capablanca) to play
New York, 1927

135   Black (Soly)

White (Golombek) to play
Antwerp, 1938

apparently interlocked position dissolves by *16.* Kt(B3) × P!, B − R3; *17.* B − Kt3, P × Kt; *18.* P − Q6, B × P; *19.* Q × B, Q × Q; *20.* Kt × Q, Kt − Kt2; *21.* Kt × Kt, B × Kt; *22.* P × P, BP × P; (the numerous exchanges have cleared the air and left White with two powerful Bishops and Black saddled with a permanent weakness on QR4) *23.* P − B3, KR − Q1; *24.* B − K3, P − KR3; *25.* KR − Q1, B − B3; *26.* QR − B1, B − K1; *27.* K − B2, R × R; *28.* R × R, R − B1; *29.* P − Kt4, B − Q2; *30.* B − Kt6, B − K3; *31.* B × B, P × B; *32.* R − Q8 ch, R × R; *33.* B × R, Kt − Q2; *34.* B × P, Kt − B4; *35.* P − Kt3 !, (not *35.* B × P?, Kt − Q6 ch) *35.* .... Kt × KtP; *36.* B × P, Kt − Q5; 37. P − R5, resigns.

TRICKS

The inexperienced player (and sometimes even the experienced) will often find that a tricky wile rather than a full-length combination has led to his downfall. Many of these tricks follow a basic and recurring pattern. Take for instance what may be called the Rubinstein trap (since that great master fell into it twice within the space of one year). In Diagram 135 Black has just incautiously moved his Kt from B3 to Q4 and White plays *12.* B × Kt, KP × B; *13.* Kt × P, winning a valuable Pawn since *13.* .... P × Kt; loses the Queen after B—B7.

The two essential factors for this trick are that the enemy Queen should be choked up by its own pieces and that a Bishop should be at hand ready to attack the Queen. See it working again in Diagram 136 where Black makes the mistake of *10.* .... Kt—R4? and loses a Pawn after *11.* Kt × P.

136 Black (Auer) to play

137 Black (Wheatcroft) to play

White (Rojahn)
Helsinki International Team
Tournament, 1952

White (Golombek)
London, 1937

A trick which the author had to learn by bitter personal experience is shown in Diagram 137. White had just played the natural developing move *9.* B—Q3? to which Black replied *9.* .... P—QKt4! *10.* P × KtP, P—B5; winning a piece. An effective blend of pin and fork that comes up quite often.

It pays to keep an open mind in all circumstances on the chess-board. For example, do not, because one always talks about a Pawn queening, assume that it may not be promoted to another piece with greater effect. Consider the following opening variation: *1.* P – Q4, P–Q4; *2.* P–QB4, P–K4; (the Albin Counter-Gambit) *3.* QP × P, P–Q5; *4.* P–K3? (correct is Kt–KB3 followed by P–KKt3 and B–Kt2) *4.* .... B–Kt5 ch; *5.* B–Q2, P × P; *6.* B × B, P × P ch; *7.* K–K2, (now if *7.* .... P × Kt=Q; *8.* Q × Q ch, K × Q; *9.* R × Q, with equality) but Black plays *7.* .... P × Kt=Kt ch and wins. For if *8.* R × Kt, B–Kt5 ch; or if *8.* K–K1, Q–R5 ch; *9.* P–Kt3, Q–K5 ch.

It pays too to retain an open mind about pins. Beware of an unprotected pinning Queen in line with a protected Queen. See what happens in Diagram 138. White plays *19.* Kt–Q5! and Black must resign for if *19.* .... Q × Q; *20.* Kt–K7 mate.

Black (Ragosin)

138

White (Bonch-Osmolovsky) to play
Lvov, 1951

THE INITIATIVE

One final remark about the use of the combination in chess. Always remember that it is a means to an end and that that end is the obtaining or retention of the initiative. As the attacker make sure that your combination achieves this; as the defender try to meet a combination with a counter-combination that will wrest the initiative into your own hands. Consider the following little game for which the judges took the unusual step of awarding a brilliancy prize to both players in consideration of the manner in which each side caps the other's combinations.

Played at Budapest, 1952, White Geller (U.S.S.R.), Black Golombek (Gt Britain): *1.* P—Q4, Kt—KB3; *2.* P—QB4, P—K3; *3.* Kt—QB3, B—Kt5; *4.* P—K3, P—B4; *5.* P—QR3, P×P; *6.* P×B, P×Kt; *7.* Kt—B3, P×P; *8.* B×P, P—Q4; *9.* P—B5, P—QKt3; *10.* B—Kt5 ch, B—Q2; *11.* B×B ch, KKt×B; (not QKt×B; *12.* P—B6, nor Q×B; *12.* P×P) *12.* Q—B2, Kt—B3; (if *12.* .... O—O; *13.* P—B6, and the Black QKt never emerges) *13.* B×P, Kt×KtP; *14.* Q—Kt1, R—KKt1; *15.* P—B6, Kt×P; (if *15.* .... Kt—B4; *16.* Q×P, R×B; *17.* Q×R, Kt—B7 ch; *18.* K—K2, Kt×R; *19.* Kt—K5 and wins) *16.* Q×RP, Kt—B3; *17.* B×Kt, Q×B; *18.* Q×R ch, K—Q2; (not *18.* .... K—K2; *19.* Q—Kt5,) *19.* Kt—K5 ch, Kt×Kt; (White wins after *19.* .... Q×Kt; *20.* Q×P ch,) *20.* Q×R,

Black (Golombek) to play

139

White (Geller)

20. .... Kt—B6 ch! *21.* P×Kt, Q×R ch; *22.* K—K2, Q—Kt7 ch; Drawn by perpetual check; for if *23.* K—B1, Q—Kt8 ch; *24.* K—Kt2, Q—Kt3 ch; *25.* K—R3, Q—R4 ch, etc.

CHAPTER 6

THE MIDDLE GAME: PLANNING AND POSITION PLAY

CHESS is a logical game in which drifting from move to move is sure to lead to disaster. It is vitally important to form a plan of campaign, and this plan must not be a mere trap or calculation of a fixed number of moves (which is one definition of a combination); but it must be a plan based on the essential nature of the position.

For example, you control the centre and can utilize this to assemble your pieces on the K side for attack on the King; whilst your opponent is hampered in his attempts to bring over his pieces to defend his King since his lack of central control acts as a stumbling block. Or, the position may hold out hopes of a Q-side attack since your opponent has a weakness there (e.g. Pawns on QR3, QKt2, QB3 = hole at QKt3). Or, he may have an attackable weakness on the K side through an ill-considered move of his KR or KKt Pawn and you can set about exploiting this. Or, all, or most, of his Pawns being on white squares, you may be able to attack him on the black squares, especially if his Bishop that moves on the black squares has been exchanged. And so on.

It might be asked 'How shall I conceive this plan?' The answer is that the plan should arise out of the nature of the opening employed, For example, in the Queen's Gambit White applies pressure on Black's Q4 and along the QB file, branching off from this to attack on the Q side; or he may take advantage of the open diagonal from his QKt1 to KR7 so as to attack the Black King with his Queen and Bishop.

Another main example is the Ruy Lopez where White puts pressure on Black's K4 and, when he has conquered the centre (or even merely blocked it), proceeds to attack on the K side.

IMPORTANCE OF THE CENTRE

This cannot be overestimated. An attack on the flank without giving due regard to the centre is doomed to expensive failure. What then happens is that the player thus attacked retaliates by striking in the centre and, other things being equal, the central attack wins against the flank attack every time. Here are two examples:

WHITE: GOLOMBEK   BLACK: ROSSOLIMO
VENICE, 1950

1.	P–Q4	P–KB4	9. O–O	K–R1
2.	P–KKt3	Kt–KB3	10. Kt–Q3	Kt–K5
3.	B–Kt2	P–K3	11. P–B3	Kt×Kt
4.	P–QB4	B–K2	12. P×Kt	Kt–Q2
5.	Kt–QB3	O–O	13. Q–B2	Kt–Kt3
6.	Kt–R3	P–Q4	14. B–B4	Kt–B5
7.	P×P	P×P	15. P–K4	
8.	Kt–B4	P–B3		

White plans to break through the centre and then obtain control of the central squares. For this purpose he concentrates his pieces in and on the centre; whereas Black has decided to attack on the Q side.

15.	....	B–K3
16.	QR–K1	BP×P
17.	P×P	P×P
18.	B×P	B–Kt1

White was threatening to win a Pawn by 19. B×BP.

19.	R–B2	B–Kt4
20.	Q–B1	B×B
21.	Kt×B	Q–R4

Part of his plan of attack on the Q side; but meanwhile White can use his control of the centre so as to radiate out with his pieces for an attack on Black's King. Black would do better to keep his Queen centrally posted by 21. .... Q–Q2.

115

22. B—Q3	QR—K1
23. R(B2)—K2	R × R
24. R × R	Kt—Q3

And here he should retire his Q—Q1, though after 25. Kt—K6, B × Kt; 26. R × B, White would still have the advantage. Now White sacrifices a Pawn to bring his Rook first to the very centre and then over to the K side to attack the King.

25. R—K5	Q × RP
26. R—KR5	

Threatening mate by Kt—Kt6.

26.	B—B2
27. R × P ch	K—Kt1
28. Q—B1	

Again threatening mate, this time by 29. R—R8 ch, K × R; 30. Q—R3 ch, B—R4; 31. Q × B ch, K—Kt1; 32. B—R7 ch, K—R1; 33. Kt—Kt6.

28.	R—K1
29. R—R4	Kt—K5

Otherwise there comes 30. B—R7 ch, K—R1; 31. B—Kt1 dis ch, or 30. .... K—B1; 31. Kt—Kt6 mate.

Black (Rossolimo)

140

White (Golombek) to play

30. Kt—Kt6

Winning the Queen for two minor pieces after which Black can last only a few more moves.

30.	B×Kt	35. R−K4	R−KB1
31. B−B4 ch	Q×B	36. R−K7	Kt−Kt4
32. Q×Q ch	B−B2	37. P−R4	Kt−R6 ch
33. Q−Q3	Kt−Kt4	38. K−R2	Kt−B7
34. R−Kt4	Kt−R2	39. Q−B5	resigns.

Since 39. .... B−Q4; 40. Q−Kt5, R−B2; 41. R−K8 ch, forces either mate after 41. .... K−R2; 42. Q−R5, or win of a piece by 41. .... R−B1; 42. R×R ch, K×R; 43. Q−B5 ch.

Another more complicated example but one that still conveys the message that the centre is all important:

WHITE: GOLOMBEK   BLACK: PACHMAN
TRENCIANSKE TEPLICE, 1949

1. P−Q4	Kt−KB3	11. QKt−B3	Q−B2
2. P−QB4	P−K3	12. P−R3	QKt−Q2
3. P−KKt3	P−B4	13. Q−B2	R−Kt1
4. P−Q5	P×P	14. B−K3	P−QKt4
5. P×P	P−Q3	15. P×P	P×P
6. B−Kt2	P−KKt3	16. KR−B1	P−Kt5
7. P−K4	B−Kt2	17. Kt−Q1	Q−Kt3
8. Kt−K2	O−O	18. P−Kt4	B−QR3
9. O−O	P−QR3	19. Kt−Kt3	Kt−K4
10. P−QR4	R−K1	20. P−B4	Kt−Q6

Not 20. .... Kt−B5; because of 21. R×B, winning two pieces for a Rook. Black will have a distinct advantage if he can maintain his Kt on its central square; but this he finds impossible.

21. B−B1	P−Kt6
22. Q−Q2	Kt−Kt5
23. P−K5	

The central blow that destroys the base of Black's Pawn structure and so disposes of his Q-side attack.

Black (Pachman) to play

141

White (Golombek)

23.	P × P

If 23. .... Kt(B3) × QP; 24. R × B! winning two pieces for the Rook; or if 23. .... Kt—Q2; 24. P—K6, P × P; 25. P × P, R × P; 26. R × B, Kt × R; 27. B—B4, Kt—B2; 28. P—B5.

24. B × P	Q—Kt2
25. Q × Kt	Q × P

Black must lose a piece; for if 25. .... Q × Q; 26. B × Q, B × B; 27. B—Q6, B × P; 28. B × R, R × B; 29. Kt—B2, B × P; 30. P × P, Kt—R4; 31. Kt × B, Kt × Kt; 32. K—Kt2, and White wins.

26. B—Kt2	Q—Q6	34. R × R	P × R
27. Q—B3	P × P	35. Kt—B3	B—QB3
28. Q × Q	B × Q	36. Kt—Kt3	R—QB1
29. Kt—B1	Kt—K5	37. Kt(Kt3)—K2	B—B3
30. B × Kt	B × B	38. P—Kt5	B × Kt
31. B—Q6	B—Q5 ch	39. Kt × B	B—Q2
32. K—R2	QR—B1	40. Kt—Q5	resigns
33. B × P	R—B7 ch		

For if 40. .... K—B1; 41. Kt—Kt6, R—Q1; 42. B—B7.

THE K-SIDE BREAK-THROUGH

Flank attacks can be undertaken when the centre is blocked so that neither side can cause trouble there. A typical example of this sort of attack is shown in Diagram 142. Here, Yates, one of

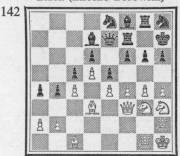

Black (Znosko-Borowski)

142

White (Yates) to play
Tunbridge Wells, 1927

the finest attacking players Britain ever had, has built up a most formidable attack out of the Ruy Lopez. The break-through came by *40.* P−Kt5, B×Kt; (if *40.* .... BP×P; *41.* Kt×P ch, P×Kt; *42.* P×P dis ch, K−Kt2; *43.* Kt−R5 ch, P×Kt; *44.* Q×P, followed by mate on R7) *41.* P−B5! (not *41.* R×B, BP×P; *42.* RP×P, Q×P!) *41.* .... RP×P; *42.* P×P, R(Kt1)−Kt2; *43.* R×B ch, K−Kt1; *44.* BP×P, R×P; *45.* Kt−B5, Q−Q2; *46.* R−Kt2, P×P; (if *46.* .... R−R2; *47.* R(Kt2)−R2, R×R; *48.* Q×R, B−Kt2; *49.* Kt−R6 ch, followed by Q×Q) *47.* R(Kt2)−R2, B−Kt2; *48.* R×Kt ch!, B×R; *49.* Q−R5, R(B2)−B3; *50.* Q×B ch, K−B2; *51.* R−R7 ch, resigns.

THE Q-SIDE BREAK-THROUGH

This usually arises from the Queen's Gambit or Queen's Pawn openings. Having placed a Rook on QB1 to apply pressure on the QB file the attacker advances his QKtP and, with the concentrated aid of his Q, Kt, and R, he forces a break-through. In Diagram 143, arising out of a QP opening, Black has attempted to blunt

Black (Golombek)

143

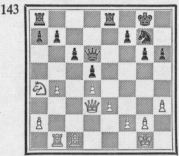

White (Capablanca) to play
Margate, 1939

the force of White's attack by numerous exchanges, but without avail, for now comes 23. P−Kt5!, P×P; 24. Q×QKtP, Kt−K3; (if 24. .... R−K2; 25. R−B5, R−Q1; 26. Kt−B3, winning the QP, and if 24. .... P−Kt3; 25. R−B6, Q−Q2; 26. R×QKtP,) 25. Kt−B3, (the most accurate continuation; Black gets counter-chances after 25. Q×KtP, R(K1)−Kt1; 26. Q−B6, Q×Q; 27. R×R ch, R×R; 28. R×Q, R−Kt8 ch; 29. K−R2, R−R8;) 25. .... R(K1)−Q1; 26. Q×KtP, Q−R6; 27. Kt×P, Q×RP; 28. Kt−Kt4, Q−R5; 29. Kt−B6, resigns, as White not only threatens Kt×R but also R−R1 winning the Queen.

PAWNS

Pawns play a special part in positional manoeuvring. When Philidor remarked that 'Pawns are the soul of chess' he was not being over-emphatic. The nature of the Pawn structure is all-important in determining what plan of campaign must be employed. The result of a game very often indeed hangs upon the existence of a weak or strong Pawn.

Pawns are strong when they are connected in a chain; when they need no defence from pieces since they are supported by Pawns in turn; and when they constitute a wedge in the enemy position. In view of their potential value, the nearer they get to the 8th rank the more menacing they are to the enemy and the greater their intrinsic worth. Pawns are weak when the reverse of the above is true; when their original formation has been broken up and they have become isolated or doubled so that they require protection from pieces of higher value than Pawns. They also tend to lose their effectiveness when blocked by opposing Pawns or pieces, especially when this means they are permanently hindered from advancing.

An ideally strong Pawn structure is shown in Diagram 144

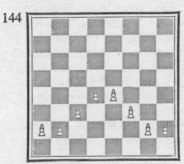

144

A strong Pawn chain

where the Pawns present an aesthetic picture of cooperation and also of central power; Diagram 145, on the other hand, shows White suffering from three defects in his Pawn structure. His QRP is isolated and will need defence against enemy attacks; still worse is the position on the QB file where his Pawns are both doubled and isolated. Not only are they objects for attack but they have little means of repelling enemy pieces. So they constitute a mute invitation to the opponent to post his Kt on QB5, or QB4, whence it will exert a most depressing influence on White's game. If one of the QB Pawns were on QKt2 then the

145

White has a weak Pawn position

enemy piece could be repulsed by either P—QKt3 or P—QKt4. At first sight White's K side presents a happier picture since there is a connected Pawn chain; but the backward Pawn on KKt2 constitutes a grave weakness. Like the isolated Pawn, it is open to enemy attack without being able to call in aid from its fellow Pawns, and there is a nasty hole on KKt3, a hole which is fixed by Black's KRP and which may well prove fatal if Black succeeds in establishing a piece there.

If an isolated Pawn on the flank is a weakness, this is much more seriously the case when the isolated Pawn is in the centre.

146

The isolated central Pawn

For there it impedes the action of its own pieces and forms a permanent object of attack for the opposing forces. The typical example appears in Diagram 146. Since the QP is isolated all Black's pieces are defensive and hindered in their action; whereas White's are aggressive, especially the strong Knight on Q4. When your opponent has an isolated Pawn in the centre always aim at establishing a Kt immediately in front of this Pawn. From this point of vantage the Kt can threaten to attack a number of vulnerable spots. Moreover, by virtue of its position it blockades the weak Pawn, i.e. prevents it from advancing and so deprives the enemy of opportunities for opening-up lines for his pieces.

How useful the Kt is on its central square appears in Diagram 147 where it performs a most effective tour. White played *18*. Kt–

Black (Gemzoe)

147

White (Nimzovitch) to play
Copenhagen, 1922

B5, Q–Q1; *19*. R(KB1)–Q1, B–B1; *20*. R × R, R × R; *21*. Kt–Kt3, B–K2; *22*. B–KB3, R–Q2; *23*. Kt–K2, Kt–K5; *24*. Kt–B4, B–B3; *25*. Kt × B, P × Kt; *26*. B × Kt, B × B; *27*. B × P ch, winning a Pawn and eventually the game.

The isolated doubled Pawn position that facilitates the action of the enemy pieces can be seen in Diagram 148. Black attacked

Black (Gligoric) to play

148

White (Teschner)
Helsinki Team Tournament, 1952

one of the Pawns by *11. .... Q–R4; 12. O–O*, (if *12.* Q–Q2,
Kt–R5; and if *12.* B–Q2, Kt–Q6 ch;) *12. .... B–K3;
13. Kt–K3, Q×BP; 14. R–Kt1, O–O; 15.* Q–K2, Kt–Q5;
16. Q–KB2, Kt–Q6; *17.* B–Q2, Kt×B ch; (giving White
some more doubled Pawns to worry about) *18.* P×Kt, Q–Q5;
19. Q–R4, Kt×P; *20.* Q×Kt, Q×B; (White's doubled Pawns
have disappeared, but only at the cost of losing two; Black now
finishes off the game with great vigour) *21.* R–B2, Q–Q5;
22. R×P, QR–Kt1; *23.* R×KP, P–Kt4; *24.* Q×KtP ch,
K–R1; *25.* Kt–B2, B–R6!; White resigns, for if *26.* Q–B1,
R–Kt1 ch; wins and in addition Black threatens both R–Kt8
ch and R–Kt1.

The dead weight of backward Pawns is fatal to Black in
Diagram 149. White, having weakened Black on both sides of the
board, now proceeds to the kill. *21.* Q–R3, Kt–K3; (the
QRP must go, for if Q–Kt2; *22.* Kt×RP, and if P–R3;
22. Kt–R7, followed by Kt–B6 ch) *22.* Kt×Kt, P×Kt;
23. Q×P, Q–KB2; *24.* R–B1, R–R1; *25.* Q×BP, R×P;
26. Q×KtP, Q–R2; *27.* Q–Kt4, R–R3; *28.* R–B5, R–Kt3;
29. Q–B3, R–B2; *30.* P–QKt4, R–R3; *31.* P–Kt5, R–R7;
32. R–B6, Q–K2; *33.* P–Kt6, Q–Kt2; *34.* R×P, Q–R3;

Black (Flohr)

149

White (Boleslavsky) to play
Budapest, 1950

35. Q–K3, K–Kt2; (to prevent *36.* Q–R6) *36.* R–KB6,
R–Kt2; (or *36.* .... R×R; *37.* P×R ch, K×P; *38.* Q–K5 ch,
K–B2; *39.* Q–B7 ch followed by P–Kt7) *37.* R–Kt1,
resigns.

THE DYNAMIC PAWN

Nimzovitch, a witty and original writer on the game, has used the
picturesque phrase 'lust to expand' about the Pawn's will to
advance and its menacing quality when well up the board. Whilst
it is prudent to keep back one's Pawns when defending, it
frequently happens that only a vigorous Pawn thrust can force
through an attack. Consider the position in Diagram 150 where
White has a fine Pawn centre but one that is under some pressure.
He played *14.* P–Q5!, B×R; *15.* Q×B, P–B3; *16.* B–KR6,
Q–Kt3 ch; *17.* K–R1, KR–Q1; (B–Q2 was a better defence;
the Bishops are so powerful here that it is not worth clinging on
to the exchange) *18.* R–QKt1, Q–B4; *19.* B–Q2, P–Kt3;
20. B–Kt4, Q–B2; (if *20.* .... Q–K6; *21.* B×P, Q×B;
22. Kt–B4, and Black's position collapses) *21.* R–QB1,
Q–Kt2; *22.* Q–Kt1, R(R1)–Kt1; *23.* P×B, Kt–B3; *24.* B–

Black (Boleslavsky)

150

White (Bronstein) to play
Moscow, 1950

B3, Kt − K4; *25.* B − Kt5, R(Kt1) − B1; *26.* B × Kt, R × R ch;
27. Q × R, P × B; *28.* B − Q7, Q − R3; *29.* Kt − Kt3, Q × P;
30. P − R4, R − KB1; *31.* Q − Kt5, R − B3; *32.* Q × R!, resigns.
After *32.* .... P × Q; *33.* P − K7, and the Pawn has gone a very
long way indeed from its original Q2.

The centre Pawns are positively invited to advance in the
following little game and accept the invitation with a vengeance.

WHITE: GOLOMBEK   BLACK: H. BROWN
LONDON, 1949

1. P − K4	Kt − KB3
2. P − K5	Kt − Q4
3. Kt − QB3	Kt × Kt
4. KtP × Kt	P − Q4

More aggressive is *4.* .... P − Q3.

5. P − KB4	P − K3
6. Kt − B3	P − QB4
7. P − Q4	P − QKt3

He should hasten to get castled by *7.* .... B − K2 and *8.* ....
O − O.

8.	B—Q3	B—R3
9.	O—O	B×B
10.	Q×B	P—B5
11.	Q—K2	P—Kt3
12.	P—Kt4	P—KR4
13.	P—B5	RP×P

Black (H. Brown)

151

White (Golombek) to play
London, 1949

14.	P×KP!	P×Kt
15.	Q×KBP	P—B4
16.	P×P *e.p.*	B—Q3
17.	B—Kt5	Q—B2

If *17*. .... B×P ch; *18*. K—Kt2, Q—B2; *19*. P—B7 ch, K—B1; *20*. P—K7 ch.

18.	P—B7 ch	K—B1
19.	Q—B6	B×P ch
20.	K—R1	

For once the discovered check does not matter.

20.	....	B—K4 dis ch
21.	Q×R ch	B×Q
22.	P—K7 ch, resigns.	

SOME WEAPONS OF POSITION PLAY

The Seventh Rank

To establish a Rook on the 7th rank is equivalent to obtaining a great advantage; to get two Rooks on that rank is deadly. On the 7th the Rooks sweep up and down destroying Pawns as they go and often threatening mate. A surprisingly large number of games are decided in this way and examples are therefore not hard to find. In Diagram 152 White tried to break out by 29. R ×

152   Black (Filip)

White (Barcza) to play
Bucarest, 1953

153   Black (Van Donk)

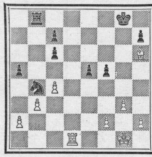

White (Spanjaard) to play
Holland, 1951

QP, but after *29. .... R × P ch; 30.* K − Kt1, R(B7) − Kt7 ch; White resigned since *31.* K − B1, R × KtP; *32.* K − Kt1, R(Kt7) − Kt7 ch; *33.* K − B1, R × KRP; would lose another Pawn and still leave him in the grip of the Rooks.

The damage can also be done by a single Rook on the 7th as in Diagram 153. White played *26.* R − Q7, Kt × P; *27.* R × BP, R × P; *28.* R − Kt7 ch, K − R1; *29.* R − R7, R − Kt1; *30.* R × P, Kt − Kt5; *31.* R × P, resigns as the KBP also falls.

What happens when both sides have a Rook on the 7th rank? Well, normally this tends to level out into a draw, but there are a number of cases in which other factors upset the balance. Diagram 154 is an omnibus version of these, adding the pin, the

154 Black (Furman) to play

155 Black to play

White (Boleslavsky)
17th U.S.S.R. Championship,
1949

Zugzwang

fork, and mating threats on the back rank so as to turn the scale in Black's favour. Play continued *38.* .... R × KP!; *39.* R − KB1, (if *39.* R × R, R − Q8 ch; *40.* K − R2, B − Q3; *41.* R − K7, R × B; *42.* R − K6, B × R ch; *43.* R × B, P − R5; *44.* R × P, P − Kt6 ch; *45.* P × P, P − B7; and Black queens his Pawn) *39.* .... P − R5; *40.* R − B8, K − Kt2; *41.* R − B7 ch, B − K2; *42.* R − Kt7 and White resigned because of *42.* .... R(K4) − K7; *43.* R − B7, P − Kt6; *44.* P × P, R − Kt7 ch; *45.* K − R1, R − R7 ch; *46.* K − Kt1, R(Q7) − Kt7 mate.

Zugzwang

This comic-looking German word means 'compulsion to move' and describes a state of affairs in which a player has no option but to make a move that brings disaster on his own head. The simplest example is to be found in Diagram 155 where Black to move must play P − R7 when White mates him by Kt − B2.

This was an end-game example; but there are subtle and charming instances where *zugzwang* occurs in the middle game and in which a player may have quite a number of moves at his disposal, but all lead to a loss.

To obtain such a position, in Diagram 156 Black made a profound Kt sacrifice by *20. .... BP × P; 21.* Q × Kt, R × P; *22.* Q — Kt5, R(R1) — KB1; *23.* K — R1, R(B1) — B4; *24.* Q — K3, B — Q6; (threatening to win the Queen by R — K7) *25.* R(B1) — K1, P — KR3; (purely a waiting move to show that

Black (Nimzovitch) to play

156

White (Sämisch)
Copenhagen, 1923

White is in *zugzwang*. Over the whole board White has only a few Pawn moves that do not lose material: P — QKt3, P — QR3 or P — KR4. All Black does is to move his King up and down until these Pawn moves are exhausted. Then White must make a losing move, e.g. K — R2, or P — KKt4; when R(B4) — B6 wins the Queen, therefore *26.* White resigns.

The Fianchettoed Bishop

Posting the Bishop on Kt2 so that it bears along the long diagonal increases its power. It has two drawbacks; the fianchetto takes two moves instead of the normal one for developing a piece, and secondly if the piece is exchanged then it is liable to leave a serious weakness on Kt2.

Nevertheless, used with discretion the fianchetto is a powerful weapon that can win many a game. Its power can be enhanced by suitable Pawn moves to clear or guard the way for the Bishop's action. When the diagonal is cleared the Bishop can deal powerful blows on both sides of the board especially when in cooperation with other pieces working on the same coloured squares. In the following game the fianchettoed Bishop comes fully into its own in the hands of a great master.

WHITE: ZITA   BLACK: BRONSTEIN
MATCH PRAGUE—MOSCOW AT MOSCOW, 1946

1.	P—QB4	P—K4	5. P—KKt3	P—KKt3
2.	Kt—QB3	Kt—KB3	6. B—Kt2	B—Kt2
3.	Kt—B3	P—Q3	7. O—O	O—O
4.	P—Q4	QKt—Q2	8. P—Kt3	P—B3

Giving the Queen an outlet to Kt3 where it can operate in conjunction with the Bishop in attacking White on the black squares.

9.	B—Kt2	R—K1
10.	P—K4	P×P
11.	Kt×P	Q—Kt3
12.	Q—Q2	Kt—B4
13.	KR—K1	P—QR4

Far as this Pawn is from the KB it also is working together with the fianchetto, as will soon become clear.

14.	QR—Kt1	P—R5
15.	B—R1	P×P
16.	P×P	Kt—Kt5

Divulging the action of the KB and preparing a fine combination.

17. P—R3?

Which combination White has not seen. His best move was 17. Kt—Q1.

Black (Bronstein) to play

157

White (Zita)

17.	....	R × B!
18.	R × R	Kt × BP!
19.	R − K3	

If *19.* K × Kt, Kt × KtP; whilst if *19.* Q × Kt, Kt − Q6.

19.	....	Kt × P ch
20.	K − R2	Kt − B7!

Now if *21.* Q × Kt, B × Kt.

21.	R − B3	Kt(B4) × KP
22.	Q − B4	Kt − Kt5 ch
23.	K − R1	P − KB4
24.	Kt × Kt	R × Kt
25.	Q × QP	R × Kt
26.	Q − Kt8	R − Q1

27.	R − R8	B − K4
28.	Q − R7	Q − Kt5
29.	Q − Kt1	Q − B1
	Threatening	Q − R3 ch.
30.	B − R3	Q − R3

White resigns.

The Two Compartments

The basis of a successful attack can often be laid by separating one's opponent's pieces into two compartments. His pieces on the one wing are sealed off by the nature of the Pawn structure and by the pressure one is exerting in the centre. Meanwhile an attack can be brought to bear on the other wing with overwhelming forces. Sometimes the enclosed pieces fail altogether to transfer themselves to the other wing and sometimes they arrive too late.

In the next example (Diagram 158) the Black Queen is shut off

Black (H. Müller)

White (Golombek) to play
Venice, 1950

from the K side for the whole game. White continued 26. B×Kt, BP×B; (26. .... KP×B; 27. R—K3, loses a piece for Black) 27. P—KR4, B—QB3; 28. B—B1, (White's pieces are all being brought over to the K side for the attack) 28. .... K—R2; 29. Q—R5, K—Kt1; (if 29. .... P—Kt3; 30. Kt×KtP, P×Kt; 31. Q×RP ch, K—Kt1; 32. Q×P ch, K—R1; 33. R—K5, followed by mate) 30. P—Kt4, R—KB1; 31. P—Kt5, B—K1; (he cannot afford to open the KR file by 31. .... P×P; 32. P×P, since he would have no defence against R—R3) 32. P×P, B—KB3; 33. P×P, B×KtP; 34. R—KKt3, R—Q2; 35. Q—R6, P—B3; 36. Kt×KP, R(B1)—B2; 37. Q—Kt6, R(Q2)—K2; 38. B—R6, Q—B3; 39. B×B, R×B; 40. Q×P, resigns – the Black Queen is still shut off from the vital field of action.

CHAPTER 7
MORE ABOUT THE END GAME

THE end game is the most important phase in chess and a knowledge of this part of the game is imperative. As far as chess is concerned the proverb 'well begun is half done' should be changed into 'well finished is wholly done'. The besetting weakness of the average amateur in this country and elsewhere is lack of knowledge in this sphere, and the standard of play would at once rise if more attention were paid to end-game study and practice.

Bear in mind that in the opening and middle game you may frequently recover from a single inaccuracy – in the end game hardly ever. Therefore study the different types of endings and try to carry out the precepts in practice as assiduously as possible if you wish to improve your strength as a player.

The elementary and basic end-game truths given in Chapter 2 should become second nature to you, and in this chapter an attempt will be made to round out the picture and fill in some of the gaps that were left when giving merely elementary consideration to the subject.

Firstly, the most powerful piece:

THE QUEEN

If the Queen was powerful in the opening and middle game its strength in the ending – when diagonals, files, and ranks are all opened wide – is enormously enhanced. It brushes aside minor pieces with contemptuous ease. Only against the Rook (which has also had its power increased greatly by line clearance) does it encounter any real opposition; but here too it nearly always prevails.

QUEEN AGAINST ROOK

Since the Queen has great checking powers it can win the Rook by a series of checks ending in a fork if the weaker side allows his Rook to stray from the King. The principle of the win for the Queen arises out of this. One brings the Queen *and King* right up to the enemy King until the latter has no move and the Rook must be detached and sent away from the King.

The typical position at which to aim is shown in Diagram 159

159

White to play

Were it Black to play he would be forced to move his Rook away from the King since *1.* .... R—Kt1; allows mate by *2.* Q—R5. With White to play he can produce the position by *1.* Q—Q4 ch, K—R1 or Kt1; *2.* Q—R8 ch, K—R2; *3.* Q—Q8. Now Black is in *zugzwang* and his best chance is *3.* .... R—R2; (if *3.* .... K—R3; *4.* Q—QB8, or if *3.* .... R—KB2; *4.* Q—Q4 ch, K—Kt1; *5.* Q—Kt2 ch, K—R1; *6.* Q—R2 ch) *4.* Q—Q4 ch, K—Kt1; *5.* Q—B4 ch, K—R2; *6.* Q—B2 ch, K—Kt1; *7.* Q—Kt3 ch, K—R2; *8.* Q—Kt1 ch, K—Kt1; *9.* Q—Kt8 ch, etc.

The method of forcing the King back to the edge of the board is as follows: (Diagram 160) Black plays *1.* .... R—KKt5; and then comes *2.* Q—B3 ch, R—B5; *3.* Q—Q5 ch, K—Kt3; *4.* K—K3, R—B4; *5.* Q—Q6 ch, K—B2; (or *5.* ....

Black to play

160

R – B3; *6.* Q – Kt3 ch, K – B4; *7.* K – Q4, R – KKt3; *8.* Q –
K5 ch, K – Kt5 *9.* K – K4, R – Kt4; *10.* Q – B6, and the Black
King must go to a back rank by *10.* .... K – R4) *6.* K – K4,
R – B3; *7.* Q – Q7 ch, K – B1; (if *7.* .... K – Kt3; *8.* K – K5,
and already the Rook must leave the King) *8.* K – K5, R – B2;
9. Q – Q8 ch, K – Kt2; *10.* Q – Kt5 ch, K – R2; *11.* K – K6,
R – KKt2; *12.* Q – R5 ch, K – Kt1; *13.* K – B6, (and now
we have a position very similar to that in Diagram 159 except
that it takes place on the other side of the board. The Rook
must leave the King since *13.* .... K – B1; loses after *14.* Q –
R6) *13.* .... R – QR2; *14.* Q – Kt4 ch, K – R1; *15.* Q – R3 ch,

Black to play

161

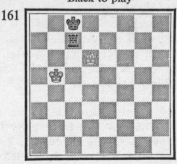

K—Kt1; *16.* Q—KKt3 ch, K—R2; *17.* Q—R2 ch, K—Kt1; *18.* Q—Kt1 ch.

But the Queen does not always win, as the player with the Rook can sometimes bring about a stalemate position. For example (Diagram 161) Black plays *1.* .... R—Kt2 ch; *2.* K—B5, (if *2.* K—R6, R—R2 ch; *3.* K × R, stalemate) *2.* .... R—B2 ch; and as the King cannot go to the Q file because of R—Q2, it can only go back to the Kt and R files when the Rook continues checking.

Queen Against Advanced Passed Pawn

The Queen has no difficulty in stopping a Pawn that has only reached the 6th rank; but what happens when the Pawn is already on the 7th rank? It all depends on what file the Pawn is placed. On the B and R files a draw is possible; on the others the Queen wins.

The winning process is to force the King in front of its own Pawn and to take advantage of this respite to bring up one's own King. Diagram 162 shows a typical winning position. *1.* Q—KB5 ch, K—Kt7; *2.* Q—Kt4 ch, K—B7; *3.* Q—B4 ch, K—Kt8;

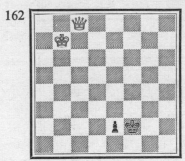

162

White to play

4. Q—K3 ch, K—B8; *5.* Q—B3 ch, K—K8; (note that the first part of White's task has been achieved by bringing the Queen as close to the enemy King as possible) *6.* K—B6.

K—Q7; 7. Q—Q5 ch, K—B7; 8. Q—B4 ch, K—Q7; 9. Q—
Q4 ch, K—B7; 10. Q—K3, K—Q8; 11. Q—Q3 ch, K—K8;
12. K—Q5, K—B7; 13. Q—Q2, K—B8; 14. Q—B4 ch,
K—Kt7; 15. Q—K3, K—B8; 16. Q—B3 ch, K—K1; 17. K—
K4, K—Q7; 18. Q—Q3 ch, K—K8; 19. K—B3, K—B8;
20. Q×P ch, K—Kt8; 21. Q—Kt2 mate.

Quite another story is told when the Pawn is transferred to the
B or R file. In Diagram 163 White can bring his Queen close by
1. Q—Kt4 ch, K—R7; 2. Q—B3, K—Kt8; but after 3. Q—
Kt3 ch, K—R8; 4. Q×P is stalemate.

163

White to play

164

White to play

The stalemate trouble also arises in the case of the RP (Diagram 164). After *1.* Q—Kt4 ch, K—R8; *2.* Q—B3 ch, K—Kt8; *3.* Q—Kt3 ch, K—R8; White is unable to move up his King because of stalemate.

Nevertheless, provided the Kings are near enough to each other, this danger of stalemate can be averted by allowing the Pawn to queen and profiting from the interval to create a mating position. Bring the King two squares nearer from Diagram 164 to Diagram 165 and White wins by *1.* Q—Kt4 ch, K—R8; *2.* Q—B3 ch, K—Kt8; *3.* K—Q3!, P—R8=Q; *4.* Q—B2 mate.

A similar win occurs against the BP as in Diagram 166 by

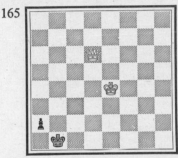

White to play

White to play

1. Q—Kt3, K—Q7; *2.* Q—Kt2, K—Q8; *3.* K—B3, K—Q7;
(if *3.* .... P—B8=Q; *4.* Q—K2, mate) *4.* K—B2, K—Q8;
5. Q—Q4 ch, K—B8; *6.* Q—QKt4! followed by Q—K1 mate.

Sometimes one may even allow the opposing Pawn to queen
with check – always provided no subsequent check is possible as
in Diagram 167. White plays *1.* K—B3, (*1.* K—Kt3, P—B8=

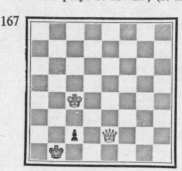

167

White to play

Kt ch and draws) *1.* .... P—B8=Q ch; *2.* K—Kt3, and Black
cannot prevent mate.

THE PAWNS

The Distant Passed Pawn

The issue of an end game often depends on whether one side or
the other can create (or has the threat of eventually creating) a
passed Pawn that is distant from both Kings. This will mean that
the defending side will have to rush over with his King to fend
off the menace whilst the other King gobbles up the Pawns left
undefended by the King rush.

A typical example is Diagram 168 where, despite the equal
material, Black is quite lost. He must play *1.* .... K—K3;
(otherwise there comes *2.* P—Kt5, P × P; *3.* P—R5, and the Black
King cannot stop the RP from queening) *2.* K—K3, K—K4;

Black to play

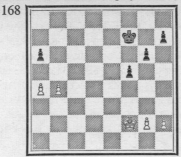

168

3. P−Kt5, P×P; 4. P×P, K−Q4; 5. K−B4, K−B4; (if 5. . . . .
P−R3; 6. P−Kt6, K−B3; 7. K−K5, and the White King gets
among the Black Pawns by K−B6 next move) 6. K−Kt5, K×P;
7. K−R6, K−B5; 8. K×P, P−Kt4; 9. K−Kt6, and Black
loses both his Pawns.

The case of two Pawns to one on the distant side (i.e. distant
from the Kings) is the simplest; but the principle holds good no
matter how many Pawns there are on the board. An example where
four to three on the Q side win is Diagram 169. White played

Black (Kramer)

169

White (Rossolimo) to play
Beverwijk, 1953

27. P—QKt3, P—QKt4; (otherwise *28.* P—B4, and White must already obtain a passed Pawn) *28.* K—B2, K—B1; *29.* K—K3, P—Kt4; *30.* P—KR3, K—K2; *31.* K—Q3, K—Q3; *32.* P—B4, QP×P ch; *33.* P×P, P—QKt5; *34.* K—B2, P—B4; *35.* K—Kt3, resigns. Nor could Black save himself on move *33.* by P×P ch; as after *34.* K×P, K—B3; *35.* P—Q5 ch, K—Q3; *36.* K—Q4, White has a simple won ending, Black being unable to utilize his three Pawns to two since two of them are doubled.

The more distant the Pawn the better, as was neatly demonstrated in the next ending (Diagram 170). Black played *49.* ....

Black (Smyslov) to play

170

White (Geller)
20th U.S.S.R. Championship, 1952

P—R4; *50.* P—QKt4, P—B5; *51.* P×BP, P—Kt5!; *52.* RP×P, P—R5!; *53.* P—B5 ch, K—Q2; *54.* P—KKt5, P—R6; *55.* P—Kt6, K—K2; *56.* P×P, P—R7; *57.* P—R6, P—R8=Q; *58.* K—Kt6, K—Q3; White resigns as he is mated after *59.* P—R7, Q—B3 ch; *60.* K—R5, K—B4; etc.

A recurring motif in Pawn endings is this quality of passing instead of capturing, and this can be seen to the full in the next subtle ending (Diagram 171). The problem is how can Black force a passed Pawn without allowing the White King

Black (Grigoriev) to play

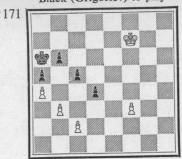

White (Subarev)
4th U.S.S.R. Championship, 1925

time to get back and stop the Pawn from queening. Black
played 56. .... P—Kt4; 57. P × P ch, K—Kt3! (not 57. ....
K × P; when Black's P—R5 would be met by P × P ch and the
White King would get back in time) 58. K—K6, P—R5!;
59. P × P, P—B5; 60. P—B4, P—Q6; 61. P × P, P × P; 62. P—
B5, P—Q7; 63. P—B6, P—Q8=Q; 64. P—B7, Q—Q1;
65. K—B5, Q—Q3; White resigns as the Black King will take
off the Q-side Pawns whilst the Queen guards the back rank.

THE OPPOSITION (DISTANT)

The straightforward type of opposition as described in Chapter 2,
page 28, is extremely important in Pawn endings, but there
exists another kind known as the 'distant opposition' that can
also be most useful. From a distance a King can (or can threaten
to) attain such a position that it will inevitably gain the normal
type of opposition eventually. The rule here is rather complicated
until one considers a specific example. When there are three or
five squares between Kings on the same file or rank the King
whose turn it is *not to move* has the distant opposition.

An example of the three-square distant opposition is Diagram

172   Black (Sajtar)   173

White (S. Szabo) to play   White to play
Bucarest, 1953

172. Had White the opposition he could force the King back and win the RP. But it is his turn to move, so that Black has the distant opposition. The Kings proceed to move sideways like Mr Winkle's horse in *Pickwick Papers* and with much the same effect: 90. K–Q2, K–Q3; 91. K–B2, K–B3; 92. K–Q1, K–Q2; (an incautious 92. .... K–Q3; would allow White to obtain the distant opposition by 93. K–Q2,) 93. K–K2, K–K3; 94. K–B2, K–B3; 95. K–Kt2, K–Kt3; 96. K–B3, and White agreed a draw as Black now has the normal near opposition by 96. .... K–B4; and then 97. P–Kt4 ch, P×P; 98. P×P ch, K–Kt4; is a simple drawn ending.

A neat use of the distant opposition to force a win is shown in Diagram 173. White wins, not by advancing his King to the third rank, but by gaining the distant opposition with 1. K–K2, K–K2; 2. K–K3, K–K3; 3. K–K4, K–Q3; 4. K–Q4, K–B3; 5. K–K5, K–B2; 6. K–Q5, K–Kt3; 7. K–Q6, K–Kt2; 8. K–B5, K–R3; 9. K–B6, etc.

MINOR PIECES

One is often met with the question: which is the better piece for the ending, the Kt or the B? The answer is that it all depends on the Pawn structure. If the position is an open one, i.e. if there are plenty of open lines along which the Bishop may travel and especially if the Pawns are not fixed or blocked but are free to advance, then the Bishop is much the better piece. Notice that in an entirely open position the Bishop can completely immobilize the Kt, as for instance in Diagram 174.

How impotent a Kt can be against a Bishop appears in Diagram 175. Black ingeniously forced off Rooks by 50. ....

174

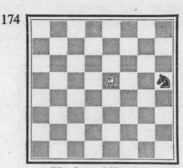

The immobilized Kt

Black (Konstantinopolsky) to play

175

White (Averbach)
18th U.S.S.R. Championship, 1950

R − Q7, *51.* R × R, B × R ch; *52.* K − K2, (if *52.* K × B, P − Kt7;) *52.* .... B − B8; *53.* P − R4, P − B5; *54.* P − B4, (otherwise Black simply marches his King up to QB7 and wins the Kt) *54.* .... P × P; *55.* Kt − B3, B − K6; (threatening P − Kt7) *56.* K − B1, B − Q5; *57.* P − Kt5, B × Kt; *58.* P × P, B − Q5; White resigns.

When, however, the position is blocked, the Kt comes into its own. The worst type of blocked position, for the side that has the Bishop, is that where his own Pawns are on the same colour squares as the Bishop, thereby impeding its movement. This is the case in Diagram 176 where Black exploits his advantage

Black (Nimzovitch) to play

176

White (Henneberger)
Winterthur, 1931

beautifully by *1.* .... Kt − K5; *2.* K − K2, K − Q4; *3.* K − K3, K − Q3; *4.* K − K2, K − B3; *5.* K − K3, K − Q4; *6.* K − K2, Kt − Q3; *7.* K − K3, Kt − Kt4; *8.* B − Q2, Kt − R6; *9.* B − B1, (if *9.* B − K1, Kt − Kt8; *10.* B − Q2, Kt × B; *11.* K × Kt, K − K5; *12.* K − K2, P − R6; and the Black King gets to either Q6 or B6; now one sees why Black wasted a move with his *3.* .... K − Q3; and *4.* .... K − B3; it was done purposely to achieve the opposition in this variation) *9.* .... Kt − Kt8; *10.* B − Kt2, P − R6; *11.* B − R1, K − Q3; (again Black wastes a tempo purposely so as to force his King through) *12*. K – K2, K – B3; *13*. K – Q1, K – Q4; *14*. K – B2, K – K5; *15*. K × Kt, K – B6; *16*. B – Kt2, P × B; *17*. P – R4, K × P; *18*. P – R5, K – R7; *19*. P – R6, P – Kt6; *20*. P – R7, P – Kt7; *21*. P – R8 = Q, P – Kt8 = Q ch; *22*. K × P, Q – Kt7 ch; *23*. Q × Q ch, K × Q; *24*. K – R3, K – B6; *25*. K – Kt4, K × P; *26*. K × P, K – K6; *27*. P – Q5, P × P ch; *28*. K × P, P – B5; White resigns.

Where the Pawns are fixed the Bishop may also be cramped by the opposing Pawns, as in Diagram 177 where the Kt is greatly

Black (Flohr)

177

White (Tartakower) to play
London, 1932

superior to the Bishop. White played *32*. Kt – B6 ch, and Black had to exchange pieces, thereby allowing White a won Pawn ending after *32*. .... B × Kt; *33*. P × B, K – B2; *34*. K – Q5, K – K2; *35*. P – QR4, P – QR4; *36*. K – Q4, K – B2; *37*. K – B3, K – K2; *38*. P – Kt4, K – B2; *39*. P × P, P × P; *40*. K – Q4, K – K1; *41*. K – Q5, K – B2; and Black resigned as White wins by P – B5.

Minor Pieces versus Pawns

When a player comes down to an end game a piece to the good he normally expects to win – but there are dangers. Beware of a position where you have a minor piece and Pawns against Pawns only and your opponent has, say, two Pawns more than you. More especially beware if there exists the possibility of your adversary creating a far distant passed Pawn on each wing.

Whilst a Rook can deal adequately with such a situation, you will often find that a minor piece is useless in such circumstances.

Black (Golombek) to play

178

White (P. N. Wallis)
Surrey Championship, 1938

See Diagram 178 where Black won by *37.* .... P—B5; *38.* K—B6, (or *38.* P×P, P×P; *39.* K—B6, P—R5; *40.* B—K6, P—Kt6; *41.* P×P, P×P; and the Bishop cannot stop both Pawns) *38.* .... P×P; *39.* P—B4, P×P; *40.* K—Kt5, P—Kt6; White resigns.

ROOK VERSUS TWO UNITED PASSED PAWNS

Whilst a Rook can normally deal with quite a number of Pawns, it must be remembered that these should not be allowed to progress too far. Against *two united passed Pawns on the sixth rank* a Rook alone is powerless. (For another example of this see page 32.) In Diagram 179 Black wins by *1.* .... P—Kt7; *2.* R—B1, P—B7; *3.* R—Kt1 ch, K—R6; *4.* K—B3, P—Kt8=Q.

Black to play

179

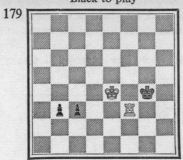

180

White to play

Even without the move the two united passed Pawns on the
sixth may win, as in Diagram 180 where White is lost whatever he
does, e.g. *1*. R − Kt1, P − Kt7; *2*. R − Kt1, P − R7; etc.

However, when the King can cooperate with the Rook by
getting in front of the Pawns there is no danger and the player
with the Rook wins.

THE KING IS ALSO A FIGHTING PIECE

Whereas the King must be hidden in the opening and protected
in the middle game, in the ending it becomes a powerful fighting

force that should be used to the full. The general rule as regards Pawn endings, or endings where less forces than Queens are concerned, is to bring your *King to the centre of operations as soon as possible.*

In Diagram 181 White has neglected this rule, whilst Black

Black (Keres) to play

181

White (Szapiel)
Sczawno-Zdroj, 1950

has brought his King right into White's camp; so that, though at the moment a Pawn down, Black wins with great ease by 47. .... Kt−K6; 48. P−B4, Kt×P; 49. P−B5, P×P; 50. P−Q5, Kt−B5; 51. P−Q6, P−Kt4; 52. Kt−B2, P−Kt5; 53. P×P, P×P; 54. Kt−K1, P−Kt6 ch; (not 54. .... K×Kt; 55. K−Kt3, Kt−K3; 56. K×P, and White draws) White resigns as he is mated after 55. K−R1, K×Kt; 56. P−Q7, K−B7; 57. P−Q8=Q, P−Kt7 ch; 58. K−R2, P−Kt8=Q.

ROOK-AND-PAWN ENDINGS

The commonest type of ending and the one that is the most often mishandled is the Rook-and-Pawn ending. To play the end game well it is essential to have a thorough grasp of the basic principles of this ending, and it is significant that the greatest masters of end-game play have been those that excelled in this particular species.

The set winning position with Rook and Pawn against Rook appears in Diagram 182. It is known as the Lucena position after a Spanish chess writer of the fifteenth century.

The Lucena position

182

White to play

The problem for White is how to obtain a shelter for the King from the Black Rook's checks without either losing touch with the passed Pawn or permitting the opposing King to approach the queening square. This is achieved by *1*. R−B4!, R−R8; (if *1*. .... K−K2; *2*. R−K4 ch, K−B3; *3*. K−B8, wins and if *1*. .... R−K7; *2*. R−KR4, followed by *3*. K−R8) *2*. R−K4 ch, K−Q2; *3*. K−B7, R−B8 ch; *4*. K−Kt6, R−Kt8 ch; *5*. K−B6, R−B8 ch; (if the Rook does not check then White plays R−K5 followed by R−KKt5; whilst if *5*. .... K−Q3; *6*. R−Q4 ch, K−B3; *7*. R−Q8, R−B8 ch; *8*. K−K5, R−K8 ch; *9*. K−B4, R−B8 ch; *10*. K−K3, R−K8 ch; *11*. K−B2) *6*. K−Kt5, R−Kt8 ch; *7*. R−Kt4, and with the White King sheltered from checks he wins.

This example shows us the conditions normally necessary for a win with Rook and Pawn against Rook. (1) *The defending King must be cut off from the queening square.* (2) *The attacking King must be able to reach the queening square* or, at the very least, *be in contact with the Pawn.*

It should be noted that much also depends on the file on

183

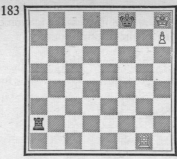

White to play

which the Pawn is placed. The most difficult is that on the R file and frequently only a draw is possible here. Just change the last position a little to Diagram 183 and we have a draw in which the previous procedure will not work as the White King cannot get out of the corner, e.g. *1.* R — Kt4, R — KB7; etc.

ROOK POSITIONS

When one has a passed Pawn the best position for the Rook is behind the Pawn, when both Pawn and Rook have added mobility and power. Conversely, when the Rook is in front of the Pawn both become immobile as in Diagram 184 where Black

184

has no difficulty in drawing. The White Rook cannot leave the Pawn; whilst if the King tries to come over to protect the Pawn then it has no shelter from the Rook checks. Black must, however, be careful where he places his King. It must stay on the second rank, since otherwise White gains a tempo with a Rook check, thereby forcing a Queen. Then, too, just move the Black King two squares along to the B file and we have the typical winning manoeuvre of *1.* R—R8, when *1.* .... R×P; *2.* R—R7 ch, wins the Rook.

This idea is often of use in practical end-game play as, for instance, in Diagram 185 where Black played *61.* .... R—R8 ch;

185 Black (Euwe) to play

White (Rethy)
Budapest, 1940

186   Black (Reicher)

White (Petrosian) to play
Bucarest, 1953

62. K×P, P—R7; and White resigned as he had no defence against the threat of R—R8.

Forcing the King to move into a position where it may be checked is also a common theme, e.g. Diagram 186, where White won by *49.* P—K4, P×P; *50.* K—R3, resigns. As White threatens mate by P—Kt4 Black must play *50.* .... P—Kt4; (or *50.* .... R—R6; *51.* P—B3!) allowing *51.* P—Kt4 ch, K—Kt3; *52.* R—Kt8 ch.

Black (Tarrasch) to play

187

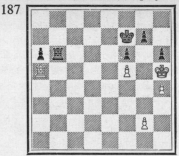

White (Nimzovitch)
San Sebastian, 1911

Rather more subtle is the next ending (Diagram 187) where, however, there appears the same theme of sacrificing a Pawn to expose the opponent's King. *33.* .... P—Kt3 ch; *34.* K×P, (or *34.* P×P ch, K—Kt2; *35.* R—R2, R—Kt4 ch; *36.* K—Kt4, P—R4 ch; *37.* K—B4, P—R4; followed by K×P and an eventual R—Kt5 ch and P—R5 for Black) *34.* .... P×P; *35.* R×BP, R—Kt1; *36.* K—R5, (not foreseeing Black's 39th move, otherwise he would have played K—R7 with drawing chances) *36.* .... R—Kt4; *37.* K—Kt4, R×R; *38.* K×R, P—R4; *39.* K—K4, P—B4 ch; White resigns, since after *40.* K×P, P—R5; and he cannot reach the QRP; whilst if *40.* K—Q4, P—B5!; *41.* K—B4, K—Kt3; and Black will capture both White's Pawns.

As a final example of how to play a Rook-and-Pawn ending I give the latter half of a game won by Rubinstein, perhaps the greatest master of this type of ending that ever lived. Note how harmoniously the whole ending flows on, and yet with what iron logic each step is taken. First, Black places his Rook in an aggressive position whilst the opposing Rook is driven to the defence; secondly, his own King is brought up to attack; thirdly, a passed Pawn is created, and finally all White's hopes are

Black (Rubinstein) to play

188

White (Schlechter)
San Sebastian, 1912

destroyed by a quiet yet crushing little Pawn move (Diagram 188). Black played *28.* .... R—K3; *29.* R—K1, (or *29.* R—Kt3, P—R5; *30.* R—B3, P—KKt4; *31.* P—KR3, R—KB3; *32.* R × R, K × R; *33.* K—B2, P—Kt5) *29.* .... R—KB3; *30.* R—K2, K—K3; *31.* K—B2, K—K4; *32.* P—B4, K—K5; *33.* P—Kt4, P—KKt4; *34.* K—B3, P—Kt5; *35.* P—B5, P—R5; *36.* R— KKt2, R—Kt3; *37.* K—B4, P—Kt6; *38.* RP × P, RP × P; *39.* K—Kt5, P × P; *40.* P × P, K—B6; *41.* R—Kt1, P—R3 ch!; White resigns.

THE END-GAME STUDY

Whereas chess problems have little or no value in increasing the strength of a chess player since they have their own artificial conventions that make the theory of the chess problem quite different from that of the game of chess, end-game studies are, on the other hand, of great use and interest to the player. They cast a bright light on the multifold resources of the various pieces and a knowledge of the masterpieces in end-game studies would increase the imaginative powers of many a player. In addition, many of the studies are entrancingly beautiful.

One of the greatest end-game composers is the Russian,

Alexis Troitsky. Many of his studies are complex and difficult, but here is quite a simple though very pleasant study (Diagram 189). White wins by *1*. B—R6 ch, K—Kt1; *2*. P—Kt7, K—B2;

A. Troitsky

189

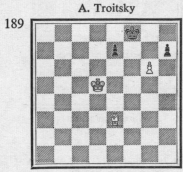

White to play

3. P—Kt8=Q ch, K×Q; *4*. K—K6, K—R1; *5*. K—B7, P—K4; *6*. B—Kt7 mate. Black had two alternatives on his second move; if *2*. .... P—K3 ch; *3*. K—Q6, K—B2; *4*. K—K5, K—Kt1; *5*. K—B6 and wins. Or if *2*. .... P—K4; *3*. K—K6, P—K5; *4*. K—B6, P—K6; *5*. B×P, P—R4; *6*. B—B2, and wins.

Another great composer was Henri Rinck of Barcelona. He produced a vast quantity of studies, and many of these are amongst the best ever composed. Diagram 190 has a most remarkable final winning move. *1*. Q—B7 ch, K—R1; *2*. Q—R5 ch, K—Kt2; *3*. Kt—B5 ch, K—Kt1; *4*. Q—Kt6 ch, K—B1; *5*. Q—Kt7 ch, K—Q1; *6*. K—Q2, and wins. For, despite the wide open board, Black is in *zugzwang*!

An outstanding contribution to the theory of K-and-P end games is to be found in the studies of Richard Réti. These also have the virtue of being most artistic. Here is a fine example (Diagram 191), where a maximum effect is produced with a minimum of material. It is one of the earliest of his compositions,

H. Rinck

190

White to play

R. Réti

191

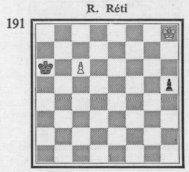

White to play and draw

having been published in 1921. The problem for White is: how is he to stop the RP from queening and at the same time save his own Pawn from capture? The solution is *1.* K−Kt7, K−Kt3; *2.* K−B6, P−R5; *3.* K−K5, P−R6; *4.* K−Q6, P−R7; *5.* P−B7, and both sides queen Pawns with a drawn ending. If on move one Black plays P−R5 then *2.* K−B6, P−R6; (or *2.* .... K−Kt3; *3.* K−K5, as above) *3.* K−K7 and draws.

Finally, one of my own favourites by a modern Soviet composer, Simchovich (Diagram 192). In this ending White cannot stop the KtP from queening, but, owing to the blocked Pawn chains, the Kt proves as strong as the Queen! He plays 1. B×P ch, P×B; 2. P—R4, P—Kt7; (if 2. ....P×P *e.p.*; 3. Kt—B3, P—Kt7; 4. Kt—Q2) 3. K—Kt2, P—Kt8=Q; 4. K—B2, Q—Kt7 ch; 5. Kt—K2, Q—R8; 6. K—K3, Q—K8; and White advances his KRP until it is captured, when he is stalemate. Naturally, Black need not play Q—K8 but other Q moves do White no damage; e.g. 6. .... Q—Q8; 7. P—R5, Q—Q6 ch; 8. K—B2, Q—B6 ch; 9. K—K1, and the Queen can do nothing against the Knight.

F. M. Simchovich

192

White to play and draw

CHAPTER 8

MORE ABOUT THE OPENINGS

THE HALF-OPEN DEFENCES

THOSE defences in which Black replies to *1*. P—K4, with some move other than P—K4 are known as 'half-open' since they tend to give rise to a mixture of open and close positions. That is to say, sometimes the centre is blocked by an interlocked Pawn chain when the play is of necessity close and at other times Pawn exchanges in the centre lead to an open position.

In this section there are five openings worth considering; firstly

The Sicilian Defence

1. P—K4	P—QB4

The Sicilian might almost be better classed as a fighting counter-attack than as a defence. Few players adopt it with the intention of achieving mere equality or of being satisfied with a draw. At the risk of certain Pawn weaknesses Black creates a counter-attack on the Q side. The Pawn structure dictates the nature of the game. White tries to establish a strong centre with complete control of his Q4. His ultimate aim is a K-side attack using an advance of his K-side Pawns as a battering ram against Black's castled King. Meanwhile Black will contest White's attempts at centre control and at the same time try to obtain a Q-side attack mainly along the QB file.

| *2*. Kt—KB3 | |

Preparing to open up the game by P—Q4; or White may plump for a close variation by *2*. Kt—QB3, Kt—QB3; *3*. P—KKt3, P—KKt3; *4*. B—Kt2, B—Kt2; *5*. KKt—K2, P—K3; *6*. O—O, KKt—K2; *7*. P—Q3, O—O; *8*. B—K3, Kt—Q5; and Black has quite a good game.

2.	P—Q3

Black's Pawn formation foreshadows development of the KB by a fianchetto, a workmanlike arrangement in which the Bishop cooperates with Black's Q-side Pawns in creating pressure on White's Q wing.

Black may also play 2. .... P—K3; and if 3. P—Q4, P×P; (otherwise White gains space in the centre by P—Q5) 4. Kt×P, Kt—KB3; 5. Kt—QB3, P—Q3; 6. B—K2, B—K2; 7. O—O, Kt—B3; 8. B—K3, P—QR3; 9. P—QR4, Q—B2; and Black will complete his development by O—O, B—Q2, and QR—B1; whilst White will try for a K-side attack by the advance of his K-side Pawns.

Experience shows that this variation is difficult for both sides since it demands extreme accuracy of play.

3. P—Q4	P×P
4. Kt×P	Kt—KB3
5. Kt—QB3	P—KKt3
6. B—K2	B—Kt2
7. B—K3	Kt—B3
8. O—O	O—O
9. Kt—Kt3	

Preventing Black from playing P—Q4; the play for some moves now circles round this theme.

9.	B—K3
10. P—B4	Kt—QR4

Not 10. .... P—Q4; because of 11. P—B5, when the QB must retreat and lose time.

11. P—B5	B—B5
12. Kt×Kt	

If 12. B—Q3, B×B; 13. P×B, P—Q4; frees Black's game.

12.	B×B
13. Q×B	Q×Kt
14. P—KKt4	Q—Kt5

193

White to play

A typical position arising out of the Dragon variation (believed by some to be so called because of a fancied resemblance between Black's Pawn structure and the shape of a dragon). Black has sufficient counter-attack on the Q side to compensate for White's K-side attack and the chances are level.

The French Defence

    1. P—K4   P—K3

Here again Black's idea is to counter-attack; but his plan of campaign is rather more subtle than that in the Sicilian. He prepares to attack White's KP by P—Q4 and even encourages it to advance to K5. Then the base of White's centre will be undermined by P—QB4 and an eventual advance of the Q-side Pawns.

    2. P—Q4   P—Q4
    3. Kt—QB3

3. P × P, P × P; leads to dull equality and an early draw; whilst *3.* P—K5, P—QB4; *4.* P—QB3, Kt—QB3; *5.* Kt—B3, Q—Kt3; gives Black a ready-made attack on the Q side.

    3. ....   Kt—KB3

Another good line is *3.* .... B—Kt5; *4.* P—K5, P—QB4; *5.* P—QR3, B × Kt ch; *6.* P × B, Kt—K2; *7.* Kt—B3, QKt—B3; *8.* B—Q3, Q—B2; with a level game.

4. B−Kt5	B−K2
5. P−K5	KKt−Q2
6. B×B	

Against Alekhine's attack 6. P−KR4, Black can simply play 6. .... P−KR3; and not 6. .... B×B; 7. P×B, Q×P; 8. Kt−R3, Q−K2; 9. Kt−B4, P−QR3; 10. Q−Kt4, when White's attack is worth more than a Pawn.

6.	Q×B
7. Q−Q2	

Or 7. Kt−Kt5, Kt−Kt3; 8. P−QB3, P−QR3; 9. Kt−QR3, P−QB4; 10. P−KB4, Kt−QB3; 11. Kt−B3, B−Q2; with equality. The idea of the Q move is that Castling K side will take some time and therefore O−O−O is contemplated.

Black to play

194

7.	O−O	13. Kt−K2	B−Kt2
8. P−B4	P−QB4	14. Kt(B3)−Q4	Kt×Kt
9. Kt−B3	Kt−QB3	15. Kt×Kt	QR−B1
10. P×P	Kt×BP	16. K−Kt1	K−R1
11. O−O−O	P−QR3	17. KR−B1	P−B3
12. B−Q3	P−QKt4		

With a level game. Note that Black's QB is forced to play a modest role here and this is the one drawback to the French

Defence. The nature of Black's Pawn formation always hinders adequate development of this piece.

Caro-Kann Defence

1.	P—K4	P—QB3

As in the French Defence Black prepares to strike at White's K4 but with the difference that no Pawns are put in the way of the development of Black's QB.

2.	P—Q4	P—Q4
3.	Kt—QB3	

If (a) 3. P—K5, B—B4; 4. B—Q3, B×B, 5. Q×B, P—K3; 6. Kt—K2, Q—Kt3; 7. O—O, P—QB4; 8. P—QB3, Kt—QB3; with a good game for Black; or (b) 3. P×P, P×P; 4. P—QB4, Kt—KB3; 5. Kt—QB3, P—K3; 6. Kt—B3, B—K2; 7. B—Kt5, O—O; 8. R—B1, Kt—B3; with equality.

3.	....	P×P
4.	Kt×P	B—B4

Best. 4. .... Kt—B3; 5. Kt×Kt ch, spoils Black's K-side Pawn structure and leaves him with little counter-chances; whilst 4. .... Kt—Q2; fails to solve the problem of development of the QB.

5.	Kt—Kt3	B—Kt3
6.	Kt—B3	Kt—Q2

Necessary to prevent White from playing 7. Kt—K5.

7.	B—Q3	

7. P—KR4, P—KR3; merely weakens White's KRP.

7.	....	P—K3
8.	O—O	KKt—B3
9.	R—K1	B—K2
10.	P—B4	Q—B2
11.	P—Kt3	B×B

12. Q × B	O—O
13. B—Kt2	QR—Q1

and the game is level; Black will eventually play P—QB4, completely freeing his position.

195

White to play

Alekhine's Defence

1. P—K4	Kt—KB3

This startling defence is based on the plan of luring White's Pawns forward so that they become objects of attack.

2. P—K5

If *2.* Kt—QB3, P—Q4; *3.* P × P, Kt × P; *4.* B—B4, Kt—Kt3; *5.* B—Kt3, P—QB4; *6.* Q—R5, P—K3; *7.* P—Q3, Kt—B3; with equality.

2.	Kt—Q4
3. P—QB4	

Or *3.* Kt—QB3, Kt × Kt; *4.* KtP × Kt, P—Q3; and Black stands well.

3.	Kt—Kt3
4. P—Q4	

164

After *4*. P—B5, Kt—Q4; *5*. B—B4, P—K3; *6*. Kt—QB3, Kt × Kt; *7*. QP × Kt, Black should ignore the QBP and play Kt—B3!

4.	P—Q3
5. P—B4	P × P
6. BP × P	Kt—B3
7. B—K3	B—B4
8. Kt—QB3	P—K3
9. B—K2	Kt—Kt5
10. R—B1	P—B4
11. Kt—B3	B—K2

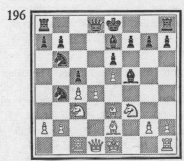

196

White to play

The position is about level; White has an imposing centre, but Black exerts great pressure on it. An interesting continuation is *12*. P—QR3, P × P; *13*. Kt × P, Kt—B3; *14*. Kt × B, P × Kt; *15*. Q—B2, B—Kt4; *16*. R—Q1, B × B; *17*. R × Q ch, R × R; *18*. Q × P, O—O; *19*. R—B1, P—Kt3; *20*. Q—Kt1, Kt × KP; and although White is nominally up in material (Q for R and B), in reality Black has rather the better chances as his pieces are working much better together and the Bishop on K6 is most powerful.

Robatsch Defence

	1. P—K4	P—KKt3

The idea of this defence, which has been practised and popularized by the Austrian player Karl Robatsch in the last fifteen years, is to try to gain control of the central black squares. It also has some resemblance to Alekhine's Defence in that Black allows his minor pieces to be chased by the White pawns in an endeavour to induce the first player to overreach himself. It should be observed that the opening move can also be made against White's *1.* P—Q4.

2. P—Q4

White's policy should be to gain command of the centre and to combat Black's pressure on the black squares. In order to retain the initiative he must play as forcefully as possible.

	2.	B—Kt2
	3. P—QB4	

This is one of four main alternatives. The others are (*a*) 3. P—KB4, P—Q3; 4. Kt—KB3, P—QB4; 5. P—Q5, Kt—KB3; 6. B—Kt5 ch, B—Q2; 7. B×B ch, Q×B; with about a level game. Or (*b*) 3. Kt—QB3, P—Q3; 4. P—B4, Kt—KB3; 5. Kt—B3, O—O; 6. B—K2, P—B4; 7. P×P, Q—R4; 8. O—O, Q×P ch; 9. K—R1, Kt—B3; 10. Kt—Q2, P—QR4; 11. Kt—Kt3, Q—Kt3; 12. P—QR4, Kt—QKt5; and Black has a good game (Hindle–Penrose, Whitby, 1962). Or, finally, (*c*) 3. P—KKt3, P—Q4; 4. P—K5, P—QB4; 5. P—QB3, Kt—QB3; 6. B—Kt2, P×P; 7. P×P, P—B3; 8. P×P, Kt×BP; 9. Kt—QB3, O—O; 10. KKt—K2, P—K3; 11. O—O, Kt—K1; 12. B—K3, Kt—Q3; with equality (Dr Euwe–Robatsch, Golden Sands, 1962).

	3.	P—Q3
	4. Kt—QB3	Kt—QB3

It is best to develop this piece straightaway. After 4. .... P—K4; 5. P—Q5, Black has difficulties in developing his Q-side pieces and the natural counter-attack by 5. .... P—KB4; gives White an advantage after 6. P×P, B×P; 7. KKt—

K2, followed by 8. Kt−Kt3. Still worse for Black in this line is 6. .... P×P; as in a game Najdorf–Robatsch, Golden Sands, 1962, which continued 7. Q−R5 ch, K−B1; 8. Kt−B3, Kt−KB3; 9. Q−R4, Q−K1; 10. P−B5, P×P; 11. B−K3, P−Kt3; 12. B−QKt5, Q−K2; 13. O−O−O, P−KB5; 14. B×KBP, P×B; 15. P−Q6, P×P; 16. KR−K1, Q−Q1; 17. Q×BP, QKt−Q2; 18. Q×P ch, resigns.

    5. B−K3

Black has good play on the black squares after 5. P−Q5, Kt−Q5; 6. B−K3, P−K4; 7. P×P *e.p.* (7. KKt−K2, would transpose to our main line as below) 7. .... Kt×P.

5.	P−K4
6. P−Q5	Kt−Q5
7. KKt−K2	Kt×Kt
8. B×Kt	P−KB4
9. P−B3	Kt−B3
10. Q−Q2	O−O
11. P×P	P×P

White has very much the upper hand after 11. .... B×P; 12. P−KKt4, B−Q2; 13. P−KR3, P−QR3; 14. O−O−O, P−QKt4; 15. P−B5 (Botvinnik–Alexander, Munich, 1958).

    12. O−O−O

And not 12. B−R6, Kt−K5; 13. P×Kt, Q−R5 ch; followed by Q×B with the better game for Black. The reader should make a note of this little combination which has a habit of recurring in positions where Black has fianchettoed his Bishop on KKt2.

12.	B−Q2
13. B−R6	

And White has rather the better game since the Black King is more exposed to attack.

THE Q-SIDE DEFENCES

In the majority of Q Pawn games nowadays Black does not reply P−Q4 but rather prefers 1. .... Kt−KB3 with the idea of contesting the centre by more indirect means than straightforward Pawn play.

One of the most popular of such defences is the

Nimzovitch Defence

1.	P—Q4	Kt—KB3
2.	P—QB4	P—K3
3.	Kt—QB3	B—Kt5

So as to prevent White from gaining control of the centre by P—K4. Much of the play in the Q-side defences is concerned with a struggle for this square.

197

White to play

Of the many possible continuations at White's disposal these are the four main lines:

Variation A

    4. P—QR3

At the expense of a doubled Pawn White forces Black to give up a Bishop for a Knight. His plan will be to advance his centre Pawns – to make his centre mobile – and use his two Bishops to the full in an attack on the King. To counter this Black must fix the centre as much as possible, blockade the Pawn position so as to give the Bishops little scope for action and eventually attack White's doubled Pawns.

4.	B × Kt ch
5. P × B	P – B4
6. P – K3	P – QKt3
7. B – Q3	B – Kt2
8. P – B3	Kt – B3
9. Kt – K2	O – O
10. P – K4	Kt – K1

With a twofold idea: (1) White is prevented from pinning the Kt by B – Kt5; (2) Black can play P – KB4 and so stop the eventual advance of White's KBP.

11. B – K3	P – Q3
12. O – O	Kt – R4

Unmasking the Bishop and preparing to attack the QBP.

13. Kt – Kt3	Q – Q2
14. P – B4	P – B4

198

White to play

Black has a good game since he has little to fear on the K side (where he will strengthen his position by P – Kt3 and Kt – Kt2); whilst White will have to take defensive measures on the other wing where Black will threaten the QBP by R – QB1 and B – R3.

Variation B (from Diagram 197)

4. P – K3

A restrained but none the less powerful line that gives the most trouble to Black.

4.	P — Q4
5. B — Q3	O — O
6. Kt — B3	P — B4
7. O — O	Kt — B3
8. P — QR3	BP × P

Also playable is *8.* .... B × Kt; but there seems no good reason why Black should so tamely give up his Bishop for the Kt here.

9. KP × P

After *9.* P × B, P × Kt; *10.* KtP × P, P × P; *11.* B × P, Q — B2; Black has excellent chances with his concealed attack along the QB file.

9.	P × P
10. B × P	B — K2

199

White to play

The chances are equal; in return for his isolated Pawn White has rather the freer play for his pieces. Possible continuations are (1) *11.* Q — Q3, P — QKt3; *12.* B — KKt5, B — Kt2; *13.* QR — Q1, Kt — Q4; and (2) *11.* R — K1, P — QR3; *12.* B — B4, P — QKt4; *13.* B — R2, B — Kt2; where, in both cases, Black has a satisfactory position.

Variation C (from Diagram 197)

     4. Q – B2

White makes a direct attempt to control K4.

     4. ....   Kt – B3

Black may also play *4.* .... P – Q4; and if *5.* P – QR3, B × Kt ch; *6.* Q × B, Kt – K5; with a level game.

     5. Kt – B3   P – Q3
     6. P – QR3

Or *6.* B – Q2, P – K4; *7.* P – QR3, B × Kt; *8.* B × B, Q – K2; *9.* P × P, P × P; *10.* P – K3, P – QR4; with equality.

     6. ....   B × Kt ch
     7. Q × B   O – O
     8. P – KKt3

If *8.* P – QKt4, R – K1; *9.* B – Kt2, P – K4; *10.* P × P, Kt × KP; *11.* Q – B2, P – QR4; *12.* P – K3, P × P; *13.* P × P, R × R ch; *14.* B × R, P – B4; with a good game for Black.

     8. ....   R – K1
     9. B – Kt2   P – K4
     10. P – Q5   Kt – K2
     11. O – O   P – QR4
     12. P – Kt3   B – B4

and the game is level.

Variation D (from Diagram 197)

     4. Q – Kt3

White tries to relieve the pin without spoiling his Pawn position.

     4. ....   Kt – B3

Black may also play *4.* .... P – B4; *5.* P × P, Kt – B3; *6.* Kt – B3, B × P; with about a level game.

     5. Kt – B3   P – QR4   *9.* P – Q5   P × P
     6. P – QR3   P – R5   *10.* P × P   Kt – QR4
     7. Q – B2   B × Kt ch *11.* P – Q6   P × P
     8. Q × B   P – R3   *12.* B – B4   O – O

with a good game for Black.

The Queen's Indian Defence

1.	P—Q4	Kt—KB3
2.	P—QB4	P—K3

Now, if White wants to avoid the Nimzovitch Defence, he can play *3.* Kt—KB3.

Black must still make it his main purpose to control White's K4 and hence he fianchettoes his Q Bishop.

3.	....	P—QKt3
4.	P—KKt3	

It is a good general rule that *when one side fianchettoes his QB the other should counter with a fianchetto of the KB.*

4.	....	B—Kt2
5.	B—Kt2	B—K2

5. .... B—Kt5 ch; *6.* B—Q2, B×B ch; *7.* Q×B, O—O; *8.* Kt—B3, P—Q3; *9.* Q—B2, is not altogether satisfactory for Black since White has gained his point in controlling K4.

6.	O—O	O—O
7.	Kt—B3	

White threatens to play Q—B2 and Black must now decide how he is going to contest the square K4.

Black to play

200

There are two ways.

Variation A

7.	Kt — K5
8. Q — B2	Kt × Kt
9. Q × Kt	P — Q3
10. Q — B2	P — KB4
11. P — Q5	P — K4

If *11.* .... P × P; *12.* Kt — Q4!

12. P — K4	P × P
13. Kt — Q2	P — K6
14. P × P	R × R ch
15. Kt × R	B — Kt4
16. P — K4	B × B
17. R × B	

and White has the better development.

Variation B (from Diagram 200)

7.	P — Q4
8. Kt — K5	

By unmasking the KB White temporarily pins the QP and Black at once takes steps to deal with this.

8.	P — B3
9. Q — R4	P — QR3
10. R — Q1	P — QKt4
11. Q — Kt3	QKt — Q2

If *11.* .... QP × P; *12.* Kt × P (B4) with advantage to White.

12. P × QP	BP × P
13. Kt × Kt	Q × Kt

and the position is equal; a possible continuation is *14.* P — QR3, Kt — K5; *15.* Kt × Kt, P × Kt; *16.* P — Q5, P × P; *17.* B × P, Q — K3; *18.* B — B3, QR — B1; *19.* B — K3, R — B5; *20.* B — Q4, QR — B1; when Black's isolated Pawn is compensated by his

173

command of the QB file. (From a game Golombek–Heidenfeld, Bognor, 1953, which ended in a draw.)

The King's Indian Defence

1. P–Q4	Kt–KB3
2. P–QB4	P–KKt3

This defence has become increasingly popular of recent years. It is emphatically a fighting defence in which Black makes vigorous use of his fianchettoed K Bishop and his Pawns to attack the black squares.

    3. P–KKt3

3. Kt–QB3, allows Black to play the Grünfeld Defence, if he so wishes; a typical line in this being *3.* .... P–Q4; *4.* P × P, Kt × P; *5.* P–K4, Kt × Kt; *6.* P × Kt, P–QB4; *7.* B–K3, B–Kt2; *8.* B–QB4, Kt–B3; *9.* Kt–K2, P × P; *10.* P × P, O–O; *11.* O–O, Kt–R4; *12.* B–Q3, P–Kt3; with equal chances.

3.	B–Kt2
4. B–Kt2	P–Q3

Partly so as to develop the QKt on Q2, but chiefly intending to strike at the centre by P–K4.

5. Kt–QB3	O–O
6. Kt–B3	QKt–Q2
7. O–O	P–K4
8. P–K4	P × P

Or Black may preserve the tension in the centre by *8.* .... P–B3; this move has the disadvantage of weakening Q3, but White will find it hard to get at this point. Meanwhile a fresh diagonal of development has been opened up for the Black Queen.

9. Kt × P	Kt–B4
10. P–KR3	

Preparing to play B–K3 without having to fear Black's Kt–KKt5.

| 10. .... | R—K1 |
| 11. R—K1 | P—QR4 |

An important move both in defence and attack. Now White cannot disturb the Black Kt by P—QKt4 and an eventual advance of the QRP threatens to go as far as QR6. This in turn will undermine White on the long diagonal and so increase the power of Black's KB.

| 12. Q—B2 | P—R5 |

201

White to play

Black could here win a Pawn by *12.* .... KKt × P; *13.* Kt × Kt, B × Kt; but after *14.* B—Kt5, Q—Q2; *15.* Kt—B6 ch, B × Kt; *16.* B × B, White would have a won game owing to his powerful Bishop on KB6.

| 13. B—K3 | P—B3 |
| 14. QR—Q1 | Q—R4 |

With equality. Black threatens to play Q—Kt5, which White can prevent by *15.* P—R3, or even deter by *15.* B—B4. This is the sort of position (as so often in opening analysis) where the stronger player triumphs.

The Dutch Defence

| 1. P—Q4 | P—KB4 |

175

A forthright attempt to obtain control of White's K4 that has appealed to many an attacking player. Using this square as a springboard for his Kt or Kts Black aims at an attack on the K side. The drawback of this defence is that Black's Pawn structure tends to become unsound and the fact that many of his Pawns get placed on white squares implies extreme difficulty in developing his Q Bishop.

>   2. P—QB4

White can also open up the position by 2. P—K4 (the Staunton Gambit) 2. .... P×P; 3. Kt—QB3, Kt—KB3; 4. P—B3, P×P; 5. Kt×P, P—Q4; 6. Kt—K5, with good attacking chances in return for the Pawn.

>   2. ....   P—K3
>   3. P—KKt3

The KB is very well placed on the long diagonal in this opening. White should not develop his QKt too early as Black can then usefully pin it with his KB, following this up with Kt—KB3 threatening Kt—K5.

>   3. ....   Kt—KB3
>   4. B—Kt2   B—K2

If 4. .... B—Kt5 ch; 5. B—Q2, B×B ch; 6. Q×B, O—O; 7. Kt—QB3, followed by Q—B2 with advantage to White.

>   5. Kt—QB3   O—O
>   6. Kt—B3

A good alternative that keeps the diagonal open for his KB is 6. P—K3, and if 6. .... P—Q3 or P—Q4; 7. KKt—K2.

After the last move Black can choose between two main lines. See diagram 202.

Variation A

>   6. ....   P—Q4

The Stonewall variation with which Black seeks to block the

Black to play

202

centre. It contains attacking possibilities for Black but suffers from two basic defects: (1) An unsound Pawn formation (hole on K4), (2) difficulty of QB development (yet another Pawn on the white squares).

7. O—O	P—B3
8. P—Kt3	QKt—Q2
9. Q—B2	Q—K1
10. B—B4	Q—R4
11. QR—Q1	K—R1

and, as Black cannot satisfactorily develop his QB, White has the better game.

Variation B (see Diagram 202)

6.	P—Q3

Here too Black has difficulties with his QB.

7. O—O	Q—K1

Or 7. .... QKt—Q2; 8. Q—B2, P—KKt3; 9. P—K4, with much the better game for White.

8. P—Kt3	Q—R4
9. B—QR3	

The best method of developing this piece.

9.	QKt – Q2
10. Q – B2	P – KKt4
11. QR – K1	P – Kt5
12. Kt – Q2	R – B2
13. P – B4	

and White will continue with P – K4 to his considerable advantage.

MORE K-SIDE OPENINGS

Ruy Lopez

In Chapter 3 the most important variation of this opening was described; but there are other main lines that are often seen. The variation given in Chapter 3 was the close line of the Morphy Defence. There is also an open line as follows:

1. P – K4	P – K4
2. Kt – KB3	Kt – QB3
3. B – Kt5	P – QR3
4. B – R4	Kt – B3
5. O – O	Kt × P

This capture, and White's reply, clear the air in the centre in marked contrast to the interlocked Pawn position in the close line.

6. P – Q4

The best move. Other lines allow Black easy equality; e.g. *6.* Q – K2, Kt – B4; *7.* B × Kt, QP × B; *8.* Kt × P, B – K2; or *6.* B × Kt, QP × B; *7.* Q – K2, Kt – B4; *8.* P – Q4, Kt – K3; *9.* P × P, Kt – Q5.

6.	P – QKt4
7. B – Kt3	P – Q4

If *7.* .... P × P; *8.* R – K1, P – Q4; *9.* B × P, Q × B; *10.* Kt – B3, and Black's position is most insecure.

8. P × P	B – K3

See diagram 203.

9. Q – K2

The modern line which vacates Q1 for the K Rook and prepares

203

White to play

to break open the position by P—QB4. Formerly the standard move was 9. P—B3, and if 9. .... B—K2; 10. QKt—Q2, O—O; 11. Q—K2, Kt—B4; 12. Kt—Q4, Kt×B; 13. Kt(Q2)×Kt, (if 13. Kt×Kt(B6), Kt×B) 13. .... Q—Q2; 14. Kt×Kt, Q×Kt; 15. B—K3, B—KB4; 16. KR—Q1, KR—Q1; with equality.

    9. ....   B—K2

If 9. .... Kt—B4; 10. R—Q1, B—K2; 11. B×P, B×B; 12. Kt—B3, B—B5; 13. R×Q ch, with advantage to White.

    10. R—Q1

The tempting 10. P—B4, would be good for White if Black replied 10. .... KtP×P; 11. B×P, P×B; 12. Q×Kt, Q—Q4; 13. Q—B4, O—O; 14. Kt—B3, but instead Black plays 10. .... Kt—B4; and after 11. P×KtP, Kt×B; 12. RP×Kt, P×P; 13. R×R, Q×R; 14. Q×P, O—O; Black has the better game despite the Pawn minus.

10.	O—O
11. P—B4	KtP×P
12. B×P	Kt—R4
13. B—Q3	Kt—B4
14. B—B2	

and White has the advantage.

The Steinitz Defence

1.	P—K4	P—K4
2.	Kt—KB3	Kt—QB3
3.	B—Kt5	P—Q3

Black decides to set up a hedgehog, defensive type of position. The defence is solid enough but liable to lead to a constricted game for Black.

4.	P—Q4	B—Q2
5.	Kt—B3	P×P

If 5. .... Kt—B3; 6. B×Kt, B×B; 7. Q—Q3, P×P; 8. Kt×P, B—Q2; 9. B—Kt5, B—K2; 10. O—O—O, O—O; 11. P—B4, and White has the better game.

6.	Kt×P	Kt—B3
7.	O—O	

After 7. B×Kt, P×B; 8. Q—B3, R—QKt1; Black has sufficient counter-play to compensate for his broken Pawn position.

7.	....	B—K2
8.	B×Kt	P×B
9.	P—QKt3	O—O
10.	B—Kt2	R—K1
11.	Q—Q3	B—KB1
12.	P—B4	

and White commands the greater space, though Black's position is quite defensible.

Steinitz Defence Deferred

1.	P—K4	P—K4
2.	Kt—KB3	Kt—QB3
3.	B—Kt5	P—QR3
4.	B—R4	P—Q3

One of the better defences to the Ruy Lopez since it is a clear improvement on the Steinitz Defence. Black, in some variations, can unpin his Kt by P—QKt4 and so preserve his centre. This in turn means that he is not obliged to play KP×P when White advances his Pawn to Q4.

5. P—B3

Preparing to attack in the centre by P—Q4 and at the same time providing a retreat for the KB when and if it is threatened by P—QKt4.

Black to play

204

In addition to the text move White has four main alternatives:

(1) The forthright 5. P—Q4, P—QKt4; 6. B—Kt3, Kt×P; 7. Kt×Kt, P×Kt; 8. B—Q5, (not at once 8. Q×P, P—QB4; 9. Q—Q5, B—K3; 10. Q—B6 ch, B—Q2; 11. Q—Q5, P—B5) 8. .... R—Kt1; 9. B—B6 ch, B—Q2; 10. B×B ch, Q×B; 11. Q×P, Kt—B3; 12. Kt—B3, B—K2; 13. O—O, O—O; with equality.

(2) The exchange variation 5. B×Kt ch, P×B; 6. P—Q4, P—B3; (Black can also play P×P as in the Steinitz Defence, with a satisfactory game) 7. B—K3, Kt—K2; 8. Kt—B3, Kt—Kt3; 9. Q—Q2, B—K2; 10. P—KR4, P—KR4; 11. O—O—O, B—Kt5; 12. Q—Q3, P×P; 13. B×P, Kt—B5; with a level game.

(3) Simple development by 5. O—O, B—Kt5; 6. P—B3, Q—B3; 7. P—Q3, Kt—K2; 8. B—K3, B×Kt; 9. Q×B, Q×Q; 10. P×Q, P—KKt4; and Black has a good game (11. B×P?, R—KKt1).

(4) The positional 5. P—B4, B—Q2; 6. Kt—B3, P—KKt3; 7. P—Q4, B—Kt2; 8. B—K3, Kt—B3; 9. P×P, QKt×P; with equality.

5.	B – Q2

Counter-attack by *5.* .... P – B4; reacts to Black's disadvantage after *6.* P × P, B × P; *7.* P – Q4, P – K5; *8.* Kt – Kt5, B – K2; *9.* O – O, B × Kt; *10.* Q – R5 ch, B – Kt3; *11.* Q × B, Q × Q; *12.* B × Q.

6. P – Q4	Kt – B3
7. O – O	B – K2
8. R – K1	O – O
9. QKt – Q2	

Or *9.* P – Q5, Kt – Kt1; *10.* B – B2, P – B3; *11.* P – B4, Q – B2; *12.* Kt – B3, B – Kt5; with a level game.

9.	P × P
10. P × P	Kt – QKt5
11. B – Kt3	P – B4
12. Kt – B1	B – Kt4
13. Kt – Kt3	P – Q4
14. P – K5	Kt – K1

and the game (which is about even) proceeds in characteristic Ruy Lopez style, with White attacking on the K side and Black counter-attacking on the Q wing by *15.* Kt – B5, P – B5; *16.* B – B2, Kt × B; *17.* Q × B, B – Q2.

The Vienna

1. P – K4	P – K4
2. Kt – QB3	

White develops the QKt first so as to reserve the opportunity of playing P – KB4. The idea is to play a kind of King's Gambit but to add to this the development of the QKt. The drawback is that, as White has refrained from immediate attack by Kt – KB3, Black has time to counter in the centre with P – Q4 and thereby secure full equality.

2.	Kt – KB3
3. P – B4	

182

Black to play

205

Against *3*. B−B4, Black plays *3*. .... Kt×P; *4*. Q−R5, Kt−Q3; and now if (*a*) *5*. Q×KP ch, Q−K2; *6*. Q×Q ch, B×Q; *7*. B−Kt3, Kt−B4; *8*. Kt−Q5, B−Q1; *9*. P−QB3, P−QB3; with a drawn position, or (*b*) *5*. B−Kt3, Kt−B3; *6*. Kt−Kt5, P−KKt3; *7*. Q−B3, P−B4; *8*. Q−Q5, Q−K2; *9*. Kt×P ch, K−Q1; *10*. Kt×R, P−Kt3; *11*. P−Q3, B−QKt2; and though Black comes out the exchange down he is much better developed and such threats as Kt−Q5 and Kt−Kt5 give him a winning attack. (See Diagram 205.)

3.	P−Q4

Not *3*. .... P×P; *4*. P−K5, Q−K2; *5*. Q−K2.

4. BP×P	Kt×P
5. Kt×B3	

Or *5*. Q−B3, Kt−QB3; *6*. B−Kt5, Kt−Kt; *7*. KtP×Kt, Q−R5 ch; *8*. P−Kt3, Q−K5 ch; with a good game for Black.

5.	B−K2	*12*. Kt−Kt5	B−B4
6. P−Q4	O−O	*13*. B×B	Kt×B
7. B−Q3	P−KB4	*14*. Q×Q	QR×Q
8. P×P *e.p.*	B×P	*15*. Kt−K6	B−Q5 ch
9. O−O	Kt−B3	*16*. Kt×B	Kt×Kt
10. Kt×Kt	P×Kt	*17*. B−Kt5	QR−K1
11. B×P	Kt×P		

and the game is dead level.

Philidor's Defence

    1. P—K4   P—K4

    2. Kt—KB3   P—Q3

An old defence that is quite solid but yields White some ground in the centre.

    3. P—Q4   Kt—Q2

206

White to play

This holds on to the central point, K4. Other moves are inferior; e.g. *3.* .... B—Kt5; *4.* P×P, B×Kt; *5.* Q×B, P×P; *6.* B—QB4, with much the better game for White. Or *3.* .... Kt—KB3; *4.* P×P, Kt×P; *5.* QKt—Q2, Kt×Kt; *6.* B×Kt, P×P; *7.* B—QB4, B—K2; *8.* Kt×P, O—O; *9.* Q—R5, with a strong attack. (See Diagram 206.)

    4. B—QB4   P—QB3

A typical and necessary precaution; if *4.* .... B—K2; *5.* P×P, Kt×P; *6.* Kt×Kt, P×Kt; *7.* Q—R5, and if *4.* .... P—KR3; *5.* P×P, P×P; *6.* B×P ch, K×B; *7.* Kt×P ch, with a winning attack.

    5. O—O   B—K2

    6. Kt—B3   P—KR3

He must prevent White's Kt—KKt5.

    7. P—QR4

Otherwise Black gains a counter-attack by P—QKt4.

7.	KKt—B3
8. Q—K2	O—O
9. B—Kt3	

Partly in anticipation of Black's Kt—Kt3, but chiefly to prevent R—K1 which could now be answered by *10.* Q—B4.

9.	Q—B2
10. P—R3	

and White has the better game.

Petroff's Defence

1. P—K4	P—K4
2. Kt—KB3	Kt—KB3

A satisfactory line that clears up the position in the centre quickly and is a good illustration of the superiority of counter-attack over merely passive defence.

3. Kt × P

Or *3.* P—Q4, Kt × P; *4.* B—Q3, P—Q4; *5.* Kt × P, B—Q3; *6.* O—O, O—O; *7.* P—QB4, P—QB3; *8.* Kt—QB3, Kt × Kt; *9.* P × Kt, B × Kt; *10.* P × B, P × P; *11.* B × P, Q × Q; *12.* R × Q, B—B4; *13.* P—KR3, Kt—Q2; *14.* P—B4, Kt—Kt3; *15.* B—Kt3, QR—Q1; with a level game.

3.	P—Q3

Not *3.* .... Kt × P; *4.* Q—K2, Q—K2; *5.* Q × Kt, P—Q3; *6.* P—Q4, P—KB3; *7.* Kt—QB3, QP × Kt; *8.* Kt—Q5, Q—Q3; *9.* P × P, P × P; *10.* B—KB4, Kt—Q2; *11.* O—O—O, and White has a won game.

4. Kt—KB3	Kt × P

See diagram 207.

5. P—Q4

White gets little or nothing out of the pin after *5.* Q—K2, Q—K2; *6.* P—Q3, Kt—KB3; *7.* B—Kt5, Q × Q ch; *8.* B × Q, B—K2; *9.* Kt—B3, B—Q2; *10.* O—O—O, Kt—B3; *11.* P—Q4, P—KR3; *12.* B—R4, O—O—O.

207

White to play

5.	P – Q4
6. B – Q3	B – K2

6. .... B – Q3; *7.* O – O, O – O; *8.* P – B4, B – KKt5; *9.* P × P, yields Black insufficient attack for the Pawn.

7. O – O	Kt – QB3
8. R – K1	B – KKt5
9. P – B3	

Or *9.* B × Kt, P × B; *10.* R × P, B × Kt; *11.* Q × B, Kt × P; *12.* Q – Q3, Kt – K3; *13.* Q – K2, O – O; and Black has a good game.

9.	P – B4
10. QKt – Q2	O – O
11. Q – Kt3	K – R1

and we have a sharp, cut-and-thrust game with equal chances.

MORE ABOUT THE QUEEN'S GAMBIT

In Chapter 3 the Orthodox Defence to the Q Gambit was outlined. But the Q Gambit is not merely one opening and comprises many distinct lines that form a whole block of widely differing openings.

Even the Orthodox Defence can soon branch off into diverse lines.

1. P — Q4	P — Q4
2. P — QB4	P — K3
3. Kt — QB3	Kt — KB3
4. B — Kt5	

If *4.* Kt — B3, Black can free his game by *4.* .... P — B4; since White has relaxed his pressure on the Q5 square.

4.	QKt — Q2
5. P — K3	P — B3

208

White to play

The Cambridge Springs variation with which Black essays a Q-side counter-attack. Against *5.* .... B — Kt5; (the Manhattan variation) White plays *6.* P × P, P × P; *7.* B — Q3, P — B4; *8.* Kt — K2, P — B5; *9.* B — B2, P — KR3; *10.* B — R4, O — O; *11.* O — O, B — K2; *12.* P — B3, P — R3; *13.* P — R4, with the better game.

6. Kt — B3	Q — R4

Threatening Kt — K5.

7. Kt — Q2	

White takes definite steps to meet the above-mentioned threat. If instead *7.* B — Q3, Kt — K5; gives Black the advantage. Quite a good alternative is *7.* P × P, Kt × P; *8.* Q — Q2, B — Kt5; *9.* QR — B1, O — O; *10.* B — Q3.

7.	B — Kt5
8. Q — B2	

And not 8. Q — Kt3, P × P; when Black wins a piece.

8.	O — O
9. B — K2	

White must tread very carefully in the Cambridge Springs. He can again lose a piece by 9. B — Q3, P × P; 10. B × Kt, BP × B. After 9. B — R4, Black sacrifices a Pawn for a strong attack with 9. .... P — K4; 10. QP × P, Kt — K5; 11. Kt(Q2) × Kt, P × Kt; 12. P — K6, Kt — K4; 13. P × P ch, R × P; 14. O — O — O, B — KB4.

9.	P — K4

Black tries the same Pawn sacrifice as given in the last note; but this is not quite so effective here since White has gained one move in development (B — K2 as opposed to B — R4).

10. O — O	

If 10. QP × P, again Kt — K5 with excellent counter-chances.

10.	KP × P
11. Kt — Kt3	Q — B2
12. Kt × P (Q4)	P × P
13. B × P	Kt — K4
14. B — K2	

and White has rather the better game.

The Tarrasch Defence

1. P — Q4	P — Q4
2. P — QB4	P — K3
3. Kt — QB3	P — QB4

A vigorous defence that strives for free play for Black's pieces at the cost of an isolated Pawn.

4. BP × P	KP × P
5. Kt — B3	

Not 5. P × P, P — Q5; when Black really does gain space in the

centre. This idea is the principal theme of the Tarrasch – *the fight for control of White's Q4.*

5.	....	Kt – QB3
6.	P – KKt3	

The fianchetto here is very strong as the Bishop bears down on Black's weakest Pawn.

6.	....	Kt – B3

If *6.* .... P – B5; *7.* B – Kt2, B – QKt5; *8.* O – O, KKt – K2; *9.* P – K4, P × P; *10.* Kt × P, O – O; *11.* P – QR3, B – R4; *12.* B – B4, and White stands better.

7.	B – Kt2	B – K2
8.	O – O	O – O
9.	B – Kt5	

Black to play

209

Black has a counter-attack after *9.* P × P, P – Q5. This again shows us the key to the whole variation – White's Q4 – for if, instead of P – Q5, Black plays *9.* .... B × P; then *10.* Kt – QR4, B – K2; *11.* B – K3, Kt – K5; *12.* Kt – Q4, Kt × Kt; *13.* QB × Kt, B – B3; *14.* R – B1, B – B3; *15.* Q – Q3, followed by KR – Q1 with marked advantage to White.

9.	....	B – K3
10.	R – B1	Kt – K5

10. .... P—B5; *11.* Kt—K5, Q—Kt3; *12.* P—K3, Q×KtP;
13. P—B4, gives White a strong attack well worth the Pawn.

11. B×B	Q×B
12. P×P	QR—Q1
13. Kt—Q4	Kt×QBP
14. Kt(B3)—Kt5	

and White, with Q4 firmly in his grasp, has the advantage.

The Albin Counter-Gambit

1. P—Q4	P—Q4
2. P—QB4	P—K4

A violent attempt to turn the game into open channels that leads to Black's disadvantage. White's best policy is not to cling on to the Pawn but to concentrate on attaining a harmonious and effective development.

3. QP×P	P—Q5

If *3.* .... P×P; *4.* Q×Q ch, K×Q; *5.* P—K4, with much the better game for White.

4. Kt—KB3	Kt—QB3
5. QKt—Q2	B—K3

210

White to play

If instead (*a*) *5.* .... B—QKt5; *6.* P—QR3, or (*b*) *5.* ....

B—KKt5; *6*. P—KR3; or (*c*) *5*. .... P—B3; *6*. P×P, Q×P; *7*. P—KKt3, B—KB4; *8*. P—QR3, O—O—O; *9*. B—Kt2, P—Q6; *10*. P—K3, P—KKt4; *11*. R—R2, P—KR4; *12*. P—QKt4, B—Kt2; *13*. B—Kt2, with advantage to White.

6. P—KKt3	Q—Q2
7. B—Kt2	KKt—K2
8. O—O	Kt—Kt3
9. Kt—Kt5	

and White has the better game.

The Slav Defence

1. P—Q4	P—Q4
2. P—QB4	P—QB3

A sound defence that has this advantage over the Orthodox Defence in that, temporarily at any rate, the QB is not shut in.

3. Kt—KB3

White can also play *3*. P—K3, when *3*. .... B—B4; is not good because of *4*. Q—Kt3. Too simplifying is *3*. P×P, P×P; *4*. Kt—KB3, Kt—KB3; *5*. Kt—B3, Kt—B3; *6*. B—B4, B—B4; *7*. P—K3, P—QR3; when Black should have no difficulty in obtaining a draw.

3.	Kt—B3
4. Kt—B3	

Black to play

211

Or White may allow the Meran variation after *4.* P—K3, P—K3; *5.* Kt—B3, QKt—Q2; *6.* B—Q3, P×P; *7.* B×BP, P—QKt4; *8.* B—Q3, P—QR3; *9.* P—K4, P—B4; *10.* P—K5, P×P; *11.* Kt×KtP, Kt×P; *12.* Kt×Kt, P×Kt; *13.* Q—B3, B—Kt5 ch; *14.* K—K2, R—QKt1; *15.* Q—Kt3, Q—Q3; *16.* Kt—B3, Q×Q; *17.* RP×Q, and White will soon regain the QP with the better game.

4.	P×P

4. .... P—K3; *5.* B—Kt5, P×P; *6.* P—K4, P—Kt4; is a real gambit in which White's command of the centre together with his better development give satisfactory compensation for the Pawn.

    5. P—QR4

It is now necessary to prevent Black's P—QKt4.

5.	B—B4
6. Kt—K5	P—K3

6. .... QKt—Q2; *7.* Kt×P(B4), Q—B2; *8.* P—KKt3, P—K4; *9.* P×P, Kt×P; *10.* B—B4, KKt—Q2; *11.* B—Kt2, P—B3; *12.* O—O, R—Q1; *13.* Q—B1, B—K3; *14.* Kt—K4, leaves Black with the inferior position owing to the enduring pin.

7. P—B3	B—QKt5
8. B—Kt5	

Black sacrifices a piece after *8.* P—K4, B×P; *9.* P×B, Kt×P; with a very fierce attack.

8.	P—B4	12. Kt×P	O—O
9. P×P	Q—Q4	13. B×Kt	P×B
10. Q×Q	P×Q	14. O—O—O	P×P
11. P—K4	P×P	15. Kt—Q5	Kt—B3

with equal chances.

The Colle System

This is a variation of the Q Pawn in which White makes elaborate preparations for opening up the centre by P—K4 and then for launching an attack on the K side. It can be dangerous against an inaccurate defence.

1.	P – Q4	P – Q4
2.	Kt – KB3	Kt – KB3
3.	P – K3	P – KKt3

212

White to play

The safest and indeed the most aggressive reply. It has the great virtue of nullifying the action of White's K Bishop, which is by far the most dangerous minor piece in the Colle system. Other good lines are (*a*) 3. .... B – B4; *4.* B – Q3, P – K3; and (*b*) 3. .... P – K3; *4.* QKt – Q2, P – B4; *5.* P – B3, QKt – Q2; *6.* B – Q3, B – Q3; *7.* O – O, O – O; *8.* P × P, B × P; *9.* P – K4, Q – B2; with a level game.

4.	P – B3	B – Kt2	*8.* Q – K2	P – Kt3
5.	QKt – Q2	P – B4	*9.* P – K4	QP × P
6.	B – Q3	QKt – Q2	*10.* Kt × P	P × P
7.	O – O	O – O	*11.* Kt × P	B – Kt2

and, if anything, Black's game is to be preferred.

THE MODERN SYSTEMS OF OPENING

For the most part, the openings discussed hitherto have been concerned with direct attempts at occupation of the centre or demolition of that of the opponent. Here and there (as for instance in the Ruy Lopez and the Queen's Gambit) indirect methods have crept in. For the drawback about direct cut-and-thrust moves in the opening is that, though they may be commendably full of vigour, they tend to equalize out all too soon. Many an open game fades away into a draw almost before the book lines are left.

Hence modern masters have sought for more indirect ways of approaching the problem of the centre and in so doing have evolved a number of new openings in which the emphasis is on observation rather than occupation of the centre.

The English Opening

Nominally this is no new opening, since it was popular in English chess over a hundred years ago. But the ideas animating it nowadays are utterly different from those that prevailed in the early nineteenth century.

1. P—QB4	P—K4

The most clear-cut reply. Quite a good system of defence also is a transposition into a kind of King's Indian by *1*. .... Kt—KB3; *2*. Kt—QB3, P—Q4; *3*. P × P, Kt × P; *4*. P—KKt3, P—QB4; *5*. B—Kt2, Kt × Kt; *6*. KtP × Kt, P—KKt3; *7*. Kt—B3, B—Kt2; *8*. O—O, Kt—B3.

2. Kt—QB3	Kt—KB3
3. P—KKt3	

It will be observed that all White's endeavours are concentrated on a conquest of the white squares and in especial Black's Q4.

3.	P—Q4
4. P × P	Kt × P
5. B—Kt2	Kt—Kt3
6. Kt—B3	(See diagram 213.)

I have worked out and practised in many a tournament an even more indirect method of bringing pressure to bear on the

Black to play

213

centre; viz. *6.* P—Q3, Kt—B3; *7.* Kt—R3, B—K2; *8.* O—O, O—O; *9.* P—B4, R—Kt1; *10.* Kt—B2, P—B3; *11.* B—K3, B—K3; but this line is perhaps too artificial and complicated to suit the general taste.

6.	Kt—B3
7. O—O	B—K2
8. P—Q3	

Or first *8.* P—QR4, to which Black in turn should reply P—QR4.

8.	O—O
9. B—K3	B—K3
10. R—B1	P—B3
11. Kt—QR4	Q—Q2
12. Kt—B5	B×Kt
13. B×B	KR—Q1

and the game is about level. White has two valuable Bishops but Black's position is solid.

Réti's Opening

1. Kt—KB3

Still more insidious in its approach than the English, this opening allows Black to occupy the centre so as to create a point of attack.

1.	P—Q4

Against the less committal *1.* .... Kt—KB3; White can proceed as in the text with *2.* P—B4, or else indulge in a more restrained system and play *2.* P—KKt3, P—KKt3; *3.* B—Kt2, B—Kt2; *4.* O—O, O—O.

2. P—B4

Black to play

214

Black now has to choose between four plans:

Variation A

2.	P × P

He gives up the centre straightaway so as to get free play for his pieces; quite a good plan.

3. Kt—R3	P—QB4	*8.* O—O	KKt—K2
4. Kt × P	Kt—QB3	*9.* KKt—Q2	Kt—Q4
5. P—KKt3	P—B3	*10.* Kt—K4	B—K2
6. B—Kt2	P—K4	*11.* Kt—K3	Q—Q2
7. P—Q3	B—K3	*12.* Kt—B3	Kt—Kt3

with equality.

Variation B (from Diagram 214)

2.	P—Q5

196

White has invited this advance in the centre and promptly proceeds to exploit it.

> 3. P—K3   Kt—QB3

Or 3. . . . P—QB4; 4. P—QKt4! sapping the base of Black's centre.

4. P×P	Kt×P	8. B—K2	B—K2
5. Kt×Kt	Q×Kt	9. B—K3	Q—Q1
6. Kt—B3	Kt—B3	10. P—Q4	P×P
7. P—Q3	P—K4	11. B×P	O—O

and White has rather the better game.

Variation C (from Diagram 214)

In this and the following line Black decides to defend and maintain his centre as long as possible.

2.	P—QB3	7. O—O	P—KR3
3. P—QKt3	Kt—B3	8. P—Q3	B—K2
4. P—Kt3	B—B4	9. QKt—Q2	O—O
5. B—KKt2	P—K3	10. R—B1	P—QR4
6. B—Kt2	QKt—Q2	11. P—QR3	R—K1

The position is about equal.

Variation D (from Diagram 214)

2.	P—K3
3. P—KKt3	Kt—KB3
4. B—Kt2	B—K2
5. O—O	O—O
6. P—Kt3	P—B4
7. B—Kt2	Kt—B3
8. P—Q3	

8. P×P, Kt×P; 9. Kt—B3, B—B3; leads to equality.

8.	P—Q5
9. P—K4	P—K4
10. QKt—Q2	B—K3
11. Kt—Kt5	Q—Q2
12. Kt × B	Q × Kt
13. P—B4	

and White's game is preferable.

The Catalan Opening

This is a blend of the Q Gambit with the two previous openings in order to accentuate pressure on Black's Q4. It needs delicate handling by White since a compromise has to be made between the demands of development and the aims of positional play.

1. P—Q4	Kt—KB3
2. P—QB4	P—K3
3. P—KKt3	P—Q4
4. Kt—KB3	P × P

Or Black may refuse to abandon the centre and play 4. .... QKt—Q2; 5. B—Kt2, B—K2; 6. O—O, O—O; 7. Q—B2, P—B3; 8. QKt—Q2, but this usually leads to a passive and constricted position for the second player.

5. Q—R4 ch	QKt—Q2	9. P × P	B × P
6. B—Kt2	P—QR3	10. Q × BP	P—QKt4
7. Kt—B3	P—B4	11. Q—KR4	B—Kt2
8. O—O	B—K2	12. B—Kt5	O—O

with about a level game; for though White has the makings of a K-side attack, Black has developed all his minor pieces satisfactorily.

BASIC PRINCIPLES IN THE OPENING

(1) Develop your minor pieces as quickly as possible.

(2) Aim at controlling the centre.

(3) In the later stages of the opening try to leave yourself as wide a choice as possible whilst confining your opponent to one or as few lines as can be.

(4) No premature sorties with the Queen.

(5) In open positions get your King into safety by castling as speedily as you can.

(6) All pieces are the more effective the nearer they are to the centre – so centralize.

(7) In attack it is all-important to retain the initiative as long as possible by continually harassing the opponent.

(8) In defence rely upon counter-attack rather than on passive self-protection.

(9) If you have got into a cramped or passive position seek freedom by exchanging pieces.

CHAPTER 9

THE GREAT MASTERS FROM THE NINETEENTH CENTURY TO THE PRESENT

ANDERSSEN

ONE of the greatest combination players of all time, Adolph Anderssen was born at Breslau in Germany in 1818. There he lived and worked all his life as a mathematics teacher, dying in 1879. He won first prize at the very first international tournament ever to be held, at London in 1851, and he repeated this success at two other great tournaments – London 1862, and Baden-Baden 1870. Some of his games will always remain famous as masterpieces of combination, in especial one against Dufresne that has acquired the title 'evergreen', and the following known as the 'immortal'.

Played at London 1851 (but *not* in the international tournament):

King's Bishop's Gambit

WHITE: A. ANDERSSEN	BLACK: L. KIESERITZKY
1. P – K4	P – K4
2. P – KB4	P × P
3. B – B4	Q – R5 ch

Better is P – Q4.

4. K – B1	P – QKt4

Again P – Q4 is preferable.

5. B × P	Kt – KB3

The drawback of this move is that it deprives the Queen of a safe retreat. Rather better is *5.* .... P – KKt4; *6.* Kt – QB3, B – Kt2; *7.* P – Q4, Kt – K2; *8.* Kt – B3, Q – R4; *9.* P – KR4, P – KR3; though after *10.* K – Kt1, threatening P × P, White has the advantage owing to his strong centre.

6. Kt—KB3	Q—R3

He plans to protect his KBP by Kt—R4, thereby sinning against the rules of development in that he unnecessarily moves the same piece twice. Better is *6.* .... Q—R4; to which White would reply *7.* Q—K2.

7. P—Q3	Kt—R4
8. Kt—R4	

Dealing with Black's threat of Kt—Kt6 ch and at the same time menacing further attack on the Black Queen.

8.	Q—Kt4

If he tries to prevent Kt—B5 by P—KKt3 then White preserves his advantage by *9.* P—KKt4.

9. Kt—B5	P—QB3

He cannot win a piece by *9.* .... P—Kt3; because of *10.* P—KR4, Kt—Kt6 ch; *11.* K—K1, Q—B3; *12.* Kt × Kt, P × Kt; *13.* Q—K2, with much the better game for White.

10. P—KKt4	Kt—B3
11. R—KKt1	

Offering up the Bishop, partly in the interests of quick development and partly so as not for one moment to be diverted from his K-side attack.

11.	P × B
12. P—KR4	Q—Kt3
13. P—R5	Q—Kt4
14. Q—B3	Kt—Kt1

Otherwise White wins the Queen by B × P.

15. B × P	Q—B3
16. Kt—B3	B—B4

Hoping to hold back White's attack by threatening his Rooks, but

17. Kt—Q5	Q × P
18. B—Q6!	Q × R ch

If *18.* .... B×B; *19.* Kt×B ch, K—Q1; *20.* Kt×P ch, K—K1; *21.* Kt—Q6 ch, K—Q1; *22.* Q—B8 mate.

    19. K—K2   B×R

If *19.* .... Q×R; *20.* Kt×P ch, K—Q1; *21.* B—B7 mate; whilst if *19.* .... Q—Kt7; *20.* K—Q2.

    20. P—K5

The Black Queen is cut off from the K side so that, despite Black's enormous advantage in material, White has a won game.

Black (Kieseritzky) to play

215

White (Anderssen)

    20. ....   Kt—QR3

Black's failure to realize that White's sacrificial powers are not yet exhausted leads to a rapid mate. A better defence was *20.* .... B—R3; since if *21.* Kt—B7 ch, K—Q1; *22.* Q×R, Q—B6; *23.* Q×Kt ch, B—B1; *24.* Kt—Q5, Q×BP ch; *25.* K—K1, Q—B8 ch; with a draw by perpetual check. For some time this was held to throw doubt on the correctness of White's combination, but researches by Falkbeer and after him by the great Russian master Tchigorin, have shown that White can still win by *21.* Kt—B7 ch, K—Q1; *22.* Kt×B, B—Kt3; (or *22.* .... Kt—QB3; *23.* B—B7 ch with a winning attack) *23.* Q×R, Q—B6; *24.* Q×Kt ch, Q—B1; *25.* Q×Q ch, K×Q;

26. B—B8, P—R3; *27.* Kt—Q6 ch, K—Q1; *28.* Kt×P ch, and White will regain the exchange with a won ending owing to his Pawn majority.

21. Kt×P ch   K—Q1
22. Q—B6 ch!

A beautiful finish.

22. ....   Kt×Q
23. B—K7 mate.

MORPHY

Born in New Orleans, U.S.A., in 1837, from a family half French half Spanish in origin, Paul Morphy flashed on to the chess world like a meteor and disappeared from it just as quickly. A boy prodigy, he was already a master at the age of thirteen; but his international career was confined to the brief space of three years, from 1857 to 1859, during which period he won first prize at New York, 1857, and then proceeded to Europe where he won matches easily against Lowenthal, Harrwitz, and Anderssen, beating the last named by +7, −2, =2.*

His stay in Europe was much embittered by the fact that he was unable to induce the leading British master, Howard Staunton, to play him a match. On his return to America he gave up serious chess and endeavoured to make a career at the Bar. Paradoxically enough, his great fame as a chess player prevented his advancement as a lawyer. Too many people had heard of him as a chess wonder to take him seriously in any other capacity. This sense of being thwarted seemed to affect his mind and he remained plunged in an apathetic melancholia for the rest of his life, dying in 1884 at New Orleans.

His games demonstrate a greatly increased regard for the principles of full development in open positions. Unlike his predecessors he never launched an attack when partially developed and only when his pieces were fully deployed would he

* In matches + is used to signify won games, − lost games, and = drawn.

begin hostile operations. This, combined with a genius for combination, rendered him supreme in his brief day.

The following typical game was played at New York, 1857, against one of the leading world players of his time.

Four Knights' Game

WHITE: L. PAULSEN   BLACK: P. MORPHY

1.	P—K4	P—K4
2.	Kt—KB3	Kt—QB3
3.	Kt—B3	Kt—B3
4.	B—Kt5	B—B4

A line that has now quite gone out of fashion, the usual move being 4. .... B—Kt5.

5.	O—O	O—O
6.	Kt×P	R—K1

If 6. .... Kt×Kt; 7. P—Q4, B—Q3; 8. P—B4, Kt—B3; 9. P—K5, B—Kt5; 10. P—Q5, B×Kt; 11. P×B, Kt×QP; 12. Q×Kt, and White has the better game.

7.	Kt×Kt	

Opening up lines for Black – just what Morphy wants. Correct is 7. Kt—B3, Kt×P; 8. P—Q4.

7.	....	QP×Kt
8.	B—B4	

And preferable here is 8. B—K2, Kt×P; 9. Kt×Kt, R×Kt; 10. P—Q3, with equality.

8.	....	P—QKt4

A bad mistake would be 8. .... Kt×P; 9. Kt×Kt, R×Kt; 10. B×P ch, K×B; 11. Q—B3 ch.

9.	B—K2	Kt×P
10.	Kt×Kt	R×Kt
11.	B—B3	

A greedy move that, in conjunction with his next, forms a faulty manoeuvre handing over all initiative to Black. Correct is 11. P—B3, threatening P—Q4.

11.	R—K3
12. P—B3?	

Now that White's KB no longer controls Q3 Black can occupy this square and so hamstring White's Q-side development. He should play simply P—Q3.

12.	Q—Q6!
13. P—QKt4	B—Kt3
14. P—QR4	

Threatening to win a piece by P—R5 and so forcing Black to break up his Q side. White has made some impression on the Q wing, *but he neglects his complete development* and so cannot hope to succeed.

14.	P×P
15. Q×P	B—Q2
16. R—R2?	

A serious waste of time. He wants to play Q—B2, but over-looks the force of Black's next move. Better is *16.* Q—R6, when Black would avoid the exchange of Queens by *16.* .... Q—B4.

16.	QR—K1
17. Q—R6	

Black (Morphy) to play

216

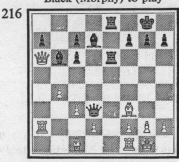

White (Paulsen)

For if *17.* Q — B2, Q × R ch; *18.* K × Q, R — K8 mate. The text move is insufficient against Black's brilliant reply. Necessary is *17.* Q — Q1.

Note how throughout the game a line that would have suited White a move back turns out to be inferior when played – a sign that Black is surpassing him both in timing and in development. (See diagram 216.)

17.	Q × B !
18. P × Q	R — Kt3 ch
19. K — R1	B — R6
20. R — Q1	

If *20.* Q — Q3, threatening Q × R; then *20.* .... P — KB4; *21.* R — Kt1, B — Kt7 ch; *22.* R × B, R — K8 ch; and mate follows.

20.	B — Kt7 ch
21. K — Kt1	B × P dis ch
22. K — B1	B — Kt7 ch

Though White has a Queen for a Bishop, the fact that at this late stage his Q-side pieces are undeveloped leaves him no chance of resistance. Black can here choose between two winning lines: the text or *22.* .... R — Kt7; *23.* Q — Q3, R × P ch; *24.* K — Kt1, R — Kt7 db ch; *25.* K — R1 or B1, R — Kt8 mate.

23. K — Kt1	B — R6 dis ch
24. K — R1	B × P
25. Q — B1	B × Q
26. R × B	R — K7
27. R — R1	R — R3
28. P — Q4	B — K6
resigns.	

Mate follows by *29.* B × B, R(R3) × P ch; *30.* K — Kt1, R(K7) — Kt7.

BLACKBURNE

Joseph Henry Blackburne, the best player this country has produced, was born in 1841 at Manchester. He learnt chess at the comparatively late age of nineteen, being induced to do so by the great fame of Morphy at that period. Throughout his long playing career the influence of Morphy could be clearly discerned in his games and one of his favourite ways of describing the brilliant and purple patches in his own play was 'a little bit of Morphy'.

When twenty-six years old he became a chess professional and soon developed into one of the most successful tournament players of the century. In match play he was not so happy, but so formidable was he in tournaments that on the Continent he acquired the nickname of the 'Black Death'. Perhaps his greatest triumph was at Berlin 1881, where he came first three points ahead of the second prize winner, Zukertort.

As a player his two great strengths were in combination and end-game skill. Dying in Lewisham in 1924, he had a total of 53 tournaments to his credit, these comprising some 814 games with a score of 62 per cent.

His games, though so strongly influenced by Morphy, also curiously foreshadow the most modern developments. For example, as early in 1883 at the great international tournament in London he was playing as Black the first three moves of Nimzovitch's Defence to the Queen's Pawn, three years before the birth of Nimzovitch; whilst his English opening at Ostende, 1907, was remarkably similar for some twelve moves to the system evolved many years later by Réti.

The vigour and force of his play is shown in the following game which he won against the then world champion in the international tournament at London, 1899:

Ruy Lopez, Steinitz Defence

WHITE: EM. LASKER   BLACK: J. H. BLACKBURNE

	WHITE	BLACK
1.	P—K4	P—K4
2.	Kt—KB3	Kt—QB3
3.	B—Kt5	P—Q3
4.	P—Q4	B—Q2
5.	P—Q5	

In a previous game between the same players at Hastings,

1895, Lasker played the more usual 5. Kt—B3, P×P; 6. Kt×P, Kt×Kt; 7. Q×Kt, B×B; 8. Kt×B, but, as in that game Blackburne outplayed his great opponent and eventually won, Lasker here chooses a less well-known continuation. Nevertheless, the committal P—Q5 is inferior to Kt—B3.

5.	Kt—Kt1
6. B—Q3	

So as to prevent Black from counter-attacking by P—KB4.

6.	B—K2
7. Kt—B3	

Better is 7. P—B4, and then Kt—B3. As played he has to move his QKt twice to a worse square.

7.	Kt—KB3
8. Kt—K2	P—B3

With characteristically vigorous play Blackburne now proceeds to destroy White's predominance in the centre.

9. P—B4	Kt—R3
10. Kt—Kt3	Kt—B4
11. B—B2	P—QKt4

Black has already made the bold and exceptional decision that his King is best placed in the centre. At the moment he is concerned with completing his development on the Q side and with breaking open the position on that wing. When this has been achieved he intends operating on the K side.

12. P—Kt4	Kt—Kt2
13. QP×P	B×P
14. P×P	B×KtP
15. P—QR4	B—Q2

Blackburne disliked playing B—B5 since it would have allowed White to obtain a strong attacking position by Kt—KB5.

16. O—O	P—Kt3
17. P—R3	

He wants to play B—K3 without being harassed by Kt—Kt5;

but the text move weakens his K side and the correct plan of development for his QB was *17.* B—R3, followed by P—Kt5.

| *17.* .... | P—KR4 |

Blackburne's amazingly sure flair for attack is shown by this immediate reaction to White's weakening move. In a very short space of time an onslaught on the K side is in full swing.

| *18.* B—K3 | P—R4 |

So as to obtain the fine square of QB4 for his Kt.

19. P—Kt5	R—QB1
20. R—B1	Kt—B4
21. Kt—Q2	

Otherwise Black wins the KP with his next move.

| *21.* .... | P—R5 |
| *22.* Kt—K2 | P—Kt4 |

A sacrifice which must be accepted since the advance of P—Kt5 cannot be allowed and *23.* P—B3 would merely create terrible holes on the K side.

| *23.* B×P | R—KKt1 |
| *24.* B×P | |

White takes too many Pawns; better is B × Kt, blunting Black's attack to some extent.

24.	B×RP
25. B—KKt3	B—K3
26. R—K1	Kt—Kt5
27. Kt—B1	B—Kt4
28. R—Kt1	R—KR1

Planning a mating attack by bringing the Queen over to the KR file.

| *29.* Kt—B3 | |

White is not content with defending himself but tries to get some counter by establishing his Kt on Q5. This is, however, the losing move in a bad position. He must play *29.* P—B3.

29.	B – KB5
30. Kt – Q5	Q – Kt4
31. P – B3	

Against passive moves Black wins by Q – R3. Now Black has an unexpected and deadly rejoinder.

Black (Blackburne) to play

217

White (Em. Lasker)

31.	R – R8 ch !
32. K × R	B × B
33. Kt × B	

He has to surrender the Queen, for if 33. R – K2, Kt – B7 ch; 34. R × Kt, Q – R5 ch; 35. K – Kt1, B × R mate.

Black now won by 33. .... Kt – B7 ch; 34. K – Kt1, Kt × Q; 35. Kt – B5, B × Kt(B4); 36. P × B, Q – Q7; 37. R(K1) × Kt, Q × B; 38. R(Kt1) – B1, Q × BP; 39. Kt – Kt6, R – Q1; 40. Kt – B4, Kt – Kt2; 41. Kt – K3, Q – B5; 42. K – B2, Q × P; 43. R – B7, Kt – B4; 44. R – KR1, R – Q2; 45. R – B8 ch, K – K2; 46. R(R1) – R8, Q – Q5; resigns as Black wins further material by 47. .... Kt – Q6 ch; 48. K – K2, Kt – B5 ch; 49. K – B2, Kt – Q4. If White plays 47. K – K2, then 47. .... Q – Q6 ch; 48. K – B2, Q – Q7 ch.

Wilhelm Steinitz, the founder of the modern school of chess, was born in Prague in 1836. He learnt and played his early chess in Vienna where he lived till 1862 when he went to England. In 1883 he left England for New York where he died in 1900.

Steinitz was the first acknowledged world champion and was equally successful in tournament and match play. In the latter he beat Anderssen, Blackburne, Tchigorin (twice), and Zukertort (twice); whilst in tournaments perhaps his greatest successes were in Vienna, 1873, where he was first and again in Vienna, 1882, where he was equal first with Winawer.

In the early part of his career he was purely a combinational player and became noted for his extremely brilliant style. But from 1873 onwards a marked change came over his play. He evolved a set of principles, a system both of strategy and tactics, that was especially useful in close or semi-close positions. Instead of an early violent clash he advocated the accumulation of small advantages; in place of cut-and-thrust play in the centre he preferred to concentrate on certain weak or strong points, and in attack he advised undermining rather than direct onslaught.

The value of his contributions to theory cannot be over-estimated. With the enthusiasm of an innovator he was naturally inclined to push things too far sometimes. He rightly said that 'the King is a strong piece' but occasionally endangered it too much on this assumption and his passion for serried defence was liable to lead to constricted positions. But, all the same, no one has influenced the progress and play of chess so much by his writings as Steinitz.

Of the wealth of games he left behind (there are 969 in the great work on him by Ludwig Bachmann) I might have chosen a brilliant example from his early career, or indeed from any period of his life. For he continued to produce brilliancies throughout his life. Instead I have selected a quieter, more positional, but still vastly entertaining and instructive game from his more mature period.

211

Sixteenth game from the second match in Havana, 1892:

Ruy Lopez, Morphy Defence

WHITE: W. STEINITZ	BLACK: M. TCHIGORIN
1. P—K4	P—K4
2. Kt—KB3	Kt—QB3
3. B—Kt5	P—QR3
4. B—R4	Kt—B3
5. P—Q3	

Instead of *5.* O—O, followed eventually by attack on the centre with P—B3 and P—Q4, White plans to keep the centre as closed as possible, whilst undertaking an attack on one of the wings.

5.	B—B4

A better line for Black is P—QKt4 followed by B—K2. As played White gets in P—B3 first of all and can then retire his Bishop to B2 in one move, instead of having to make two journeys (to Kt3 when attacked by the Pawn and then to QB2 when Black plays Kt—QR4).

6. P—B3	

Not *6.* B × Kt, QP × B; *7.* Kt × P, Q—Q5; when Black wins a piece.

6.	P—QKt4
7. B—B2	P—Q4
8. Q—K2	

A move introduced by Steinitz with the purpose of holding the centre firm. It also avoids exchange of Queens and brings extra pressure to bear on Black's KP.

8.	O—O

Against *8.* .... P—Q5; White plays *9.* QKt—Q2, threatening Kt—Kt3.

9. B—Kt5	P × P
10. P × P	P—R3
11. B—KR4	Q—Q3
12. O—O	Kt—KR4
13. B—KKt3	B—KKt5

This pin turns out to be ineffective; it would be better to develop the Bishop centrally by B−K3.

14. P−Kt4

Fixing the Black QKtP for attack. If at once *14.* P−QR4, P−Kt5.

14.	B−Kt3
15. P−QR4	P×P
16. QKt−Q2	Q−B3
17. B×RP	Kt−K2
18. Q−B4	B−K3

Allowing a liquidation that is clearly in White's favour. Preferable is *18.* .... Kt−Kt3; *19.* B−B6, B−K3; though White still has some advantage after *20.* B−Q5.

19. B×P	B×Q
20. B×Q	Kt×B

White wins material after *20.* .... B×R; *21.* B×Kt.

21. Kt×B	Kt×P
22. Kt×B	

Though this unites Black's isolated Pawns, it removes his most active minor piece and so retains the initiative.

22.	P×Kt
23. KR−K1	P−B4
24. Kt−K5	KR−B1

Not *24.* .... Kt×QBP; *25.* Kt−Q7.

25. P−QB4	R−R2
26. P−B3	Kt−KB3
27. B−Kt3	K−B1

The King is still in danger here; better is K−R2.

28. P−Kt5	P−QR4
29. KR−Q1	R−K1

Black (Tchigorin)

White (Steinitz) to play

30. P−B5!

A fine Pawn sacrifice that, by creating an advanced and mobile passed Pawn on the QKt file, forces a quick win.

30.	P × P
31. R−Q6	R−Kt1
32. QR−Q1	R(R2)−R1

He is mated if he takes the Pawn; e.g. *32.* .... R × P; *33.* R−Q8 ch, Kt−K1; *34.* R × Kt ch, K × R; *35.* B−B7 ch, K−B1; *36.* R−Q8, a variation that shows how necessary it was on move 27 for Black to play K−R2.

33. P−Kt6	P−R5
34. B × P!	K−Kt1

Or *34.* .... R × B; *35.* R−Q8 ch, R × R; *36.* R × R ch, Kt−K1; *37.* P−Kt7, and wins.

35. Kt−B6	Kt × Kt

Again R × B loses after *36.* Kt × R, R−QKt5; *37.* Kt−R6, R−Kt4; *38.* Kt × P, R × Kt; *39.* P−Kt7, R−Kt4; *40.* R−Q8 ch.

36. B × Kt	Kt−K1
37. P−Kt7	R−R2
38. R−Q8	resigns.

Making a considerable jump forward we come to the great elucidator of Steinitz's principles, Siegbert Tarrasch, who, like Anderssen, was born in Breslau. By profession a doctor of medicine, he lived and practised in Nuremburg until 1914 and then in Munich till his death in 1934.

In tournament play he was one of the most successful of all time, his career being studded with successes such as first prize at the great international tournaments of Breslau 1889, Manchester 1890, Dresden 1892, Leipzig 1894, Vienna 1898, Monte Carlo 1903, Ostende 1907, and numerous other first prizes in lesser events. In match play he was not so formidable. For, though he had resounding victories over Marshall and Mieses, he lost twice to Em. Lasker and drew matches against Tchigorin and Schlechter.

He was indeed a great player whose best games are outstanding for their strict adherence to logic and a passionate search after chess truth. Still more important was his contribution to chess as a writer and theoretician. Though sometimes over-dogmatic, by and large his works constitute an enunciation and explanation of chess principles that have never been equalled. In addition his books contain many neat and memorable epigrams such as, for instance, the following beautiful sentence from his last book, *The Game of Chess*: 'Chess, like love, like music, has the power to make men happy.'

The following game shows how, more than any other player before him, he was adept at the exploitation of command of greater space. Vienna 1898:

French Defence

WHITE: S. TARRASCH		BLACK: E. SCHIFFERS	
1. P−Q4	P−K3	*5.* P−K5	KKt−Q2
2. P−K4	P−Q4	*6.* B×B	Q×B
3. Kt−QB3	Kt−KB3	*7.* Kt−Kt5	
4. B−Kt5	B−K2		

Best here is Q – Q2 as given in Chapter 8, page 162.

7.	....	Kt – Kt3
8.	P – QB3	P – QR3
9.	Kt – QR3	P – QB4
10.	Kt – B2	Kt – B3
11.	P – KB4	P × P

He exchanges Pawns too early. Better is development of the Q side by 11. .... B – Q2; and if 12. Kt – B3, Kt – R5; 13. R – QKt1, P – QKt4; 14. B – Q3, R – QB1; and Black has a good counter-attack on the Q side.

12.	P × P	B – Q2
13.	P – QKt3	

A fine move that deprives Black's Kt of the two squares QB5 and QR5.

13.	....	R – QB1
14.	Q – Q2	O – O
15.	Kt – B3	P – B4

Black fears a possible attack on his KR2, but here, and later on, he errs through excessive caution. More active and therefore better is 15. .... P – B3.

16.	B – Q3	R – QB2
17.	O – O	K – R1

Again over-cautious. He should try to get the Bishop into play by B – K1 and B – R4.

18.	K – R1	

Whilst Black's K move was timid, this is attacking. He contemplates an assault on the K side by P – KR3 and P – KKt4 and therefore wishes to bring a R to KKt1.

18.	......	B – K1
19.	P – KR3	Kt – R2

So as to get his Kt to Kt4, but White at once prevents this. He should still play 19. .... B – R4; and if 20. Kt – R2, Q – R5.

20. P−QR4	Kt−B3
21. P−KKt4	P−Kt3
22. P−R5	Kt−B1
23. R−KKt1	Kt(B3)−R2
24. R−Kt3	P×P

Black loses patience and wrongly opens up the position. He should play B−Kt4 at once.

25. P×P	B−Kt4
26. P−B5!	B×B
27. P−B6!	Q−K1

Or 27. .... R×P; *28.* P×R, Q−Q3; *29.* Kt−K5, B×Kt; *30.* Q−R6, B−K5 ch; *31.* K−R2, K−Kt1; *32.* R−KB1, followed by P−B7 ch winning.

28. Q×B	Kt−Kt4
29. Kt−Kt5	

Apparently Black can now win by attacking the Queen with

29.	R−B6

Black (Schiffers)

219

White (Tarrasch) to play

30. Q×R

A carefully prepared sacrifice that, owing to White's greater command of space, wins in every variation.

30.	Kt × Q
31. R × Kt	P — R3
32. R — KR3	Q — B3

If *32.* .... P — R4; *33.* R — KKt1, Kt — R2; *34.* P × P, P × P; *35.* Kt × P, R — Kt1; *36.* Kt — Kt7 and wins.

33. R × P ch	K — Kt1
34. R × P ch	K — R1
35. Kt — K1	

Threatening mate by R — R2 — KR2.

35.	Kt — K2
36. R — R6 ch	K — Kt1
37. Kt — Kt2	Q — B6
38. R — K1	Kt — B3
39. R — Kt6 ch	K — R1
40. R — K3	Q × R
41. Kt × Q	resigns

LASKER

The successor to Steinitz as world champion was Emanuel Lasker, a player supremely competent in all phases of the game but most celebrated for his fighting qualities, his will to win that enabled him to snatch many a seemingly lost game out of the fire and to thread his way successfully through perplexities that would have baffled lesser masters. His contributions to opening and end-game theory were great, but he founded no school and left no especial disciples behind him.

Lasker was born in 1868 at Berlinchen in Germany. He took a degree in philosophy at Heidelberg University and his subsequent books on chess were always intermingled with (some would say 'marred by') philosophic conceptions. Turning chess professional at an early stage in life, he was outstandingly successful both in tournaments and matches. His chief tournament successes were first prize at St Petersburg 1895, London 1899, St Petersburg 1914, Berlin 1918, and New York 1924. No player has ever retained so much of his skill when old as Lasker. As late as 1935 he was third in a very strong international tournament of twenty players at Moscow. Even more formidable in matches, he crushed Blackburne, Mieses, Marshall, Tarrasch, and Janowski (amongst others), beating Steinitz in two world championship matches and losing only to Capablanca. Much of his later life was spent in England and America. He left Germany permanently when the Nazi régime rose to power and died in New York in 1941.

The following game shows him conjuring up a fierce attack almost out of nothing. St Petersburg 1909:

Ruy Lopez, Morphy Defence

WHITE: EM. LASKER   BLACK: R. TEICHMANN

1. P – K4	P – K4
2. Kt – KB3	Kt – QB3
3. B – Kt5	P – QR3
4. B – R4	Kt – B3
5. O – O	B – K2
6. Q – K2	

An attractive alternative to the more usual R – K1. Space is made for the K Rook on Q1 so as to obtain pressure on the Q file.

6.	P – QKt4
7. B – Kt3	P – Q3
8. P – B3	O – O

Black's best course is to build up a position similar to that in the normal close defence and play *8.* .... Kt – QR4; *9.* B – B2, P – B4; *10.* P – Q4, Q – B2.

9. P – Q4	P × P
10. P × P	B – Kt5
11. R – Q1	

Threatening P – K5 to force the Kt away and then play B – Q5.

11.	P – Q4
12. P – K5	Kt – K5
13. Kt – B3	Kt × Kt
14. P × Kt	P – B3

A weakening of the K side of which White takes immediate advantage. Best is *14*. .... Q – Q2.

15. P – KR3	B – R4

Forced; if *15*. .... B × Kt; *16*. Q × B, and Black cannot save the QP; or if *15*. .... B – K3; *16*. P × P, R × P; *17*. B – Kt5, R – Kt3; *18*. B – B2. Finally if *15*. .... B – KB4; *16*. P – Kt4.

16. P – Kt4	B – B2
17. P – K6!	B – Kt3
18. Kt – R4	Kt – R4
19. Kt × B	

Lasker, in his notes to the game in the tournament book points out that this exchange must be made; for if *19*. B – B2, B × B; *20*. Q × B, Kt – B5; *21*. P – B4, Kt – Q3; *22*. P – B5, Kt – K5; and White cannot break through.

19.	P × Kt
20. B – B2	P – KB4

If *20*. .... K – R2; *21*. P – KR4, followed by P – R5.

21. K – R1	

Now the Rook is to be brought over to KKt1 to take advantage of Black's weakened K side.

21.	B – Q3
22. P × P	Q – R5
23. Q – B3	P × P
24. R – KKt1	

With the immediate threat of *25*. B × P, Q – B3; *26*. Q – Kt4.

24.	P – B5
25. R – Kt4	Q – R3
26. P – K7	B × P
27. B × P	Q – K3

and Black resigned before White could reply since *28.* R × P ch, is decisive; e.g. *28.* .... K × R; *29.* R − Kt1 ch, K − B2; *30.* Q − R5 ch, K − B3; *31.* Q − Kt6 mate.

Black (Teichmann)

220

White (Em. Lasker) to play

CAPABLANCA

When in 1911 an unknown young Cuban entered for the great international tournament at San Sebastian many of the competitors protested against his inclusion in a field that contained all the great players of the day except Lasker. Nevertheless he won first prize. This young player was José Raoul Capablanca who was born in 1888 at Havana. A boy prodigy, he was playing master chess at the age of twelve when he defeated Corzo, the champion of Cuba, in a match. He was educated at Columbia University in New York and had a diplomatic career in the Cuban Foreign Office. Thus, despite his world-wide fame as a player, he never became a chess professional. He died in New York in 1942.

In tournaments he was even more successful than his predecessor in the world championship, Lasker. His first prizes included San Sebastian 1911, London 1922, New York 1927, Berlin and Budapest 1928, Budapest 1929, Moscow and Nottingham 1936. Apart from a loss to Alekhine his match

record was a series of triumphs. In 1905 he beat Marshall by
+8, −1, =14; in 1919 he beat Kostich 5−0; in 1921 he won
a world championship match against Lasker by +4, −0, =14
and in 1932 he beat Euwe by +2, −0, =8.

The clear correctness of Capablanca's play has never been
equalled; yet he won more brilliancy prizes than most masters.

Despite a somewhat limited repertoire of openings he greatly
enriched opening theory with innovations and new systems that
are imprinted with the hallmark of his dynamic simplicity.

Here is a game that seems perfectly natural once one has
played through it; but no one, save Capablanca, could have
produced it. New York 1927:

Queen's Gambit Declined

WHITE: J. E. CAPABLANCA   BLACK: R. SPIELMANN

1.	P−Q4	P−Q4
2.	Kt−KB3	P−K3
3.	P−B4	Kt−Q2
4.	Kt−B3	KKt−B3
5.	B−Kt5	B−Kt5

Inferior to the Orthodox Defence, B−K2.

6.	P×P	P×P
7.	Q−R4	B×Kt ch

More in the spirit of this defence is *7*. .... P−B4. He should
only exchange this Bishop when forced to do so by a Pawn move
from White.

8.	P×B	O−O
9.	P−K3	P−B4
10.	B−Q3	P−B5

Planning to advance on the Q side by P−QR3 and P−QKt4.

11.	B−B2	Q−K2
12.	O−O	P−QR3
13.	KR−K1	

Threatening to take advantage of the pinned Kt so as to play
P−K4.

13.	Q – K3
14. Kt – Q2	P – Kt4
15. Q – R5	Kt – K5

Preferable is Q-side development by B – Kt2.

| 16. Kt × Kt | P × Kt |
| 17. P – QR4! | Q – Q4 |

At once attacking the Bishop and defending his QKtP. Black now expects White to retire the Bishop to either R4 or B4 when he can hold his position by *18.* .... B – Kt2; but

Black (Spielmann)

221

White (Capablanca) to play

| 18. P × P! | Q × B |

He might as well accept the sacrifice; for if *18.* .... B – Kt2; *19.* P × P, Q × Q; *20.* R × Q, R × P; *21.* R × R, B × R; *22.* B × P, winning easily for White.

| 19. B × P | R – Kt1 |

If *19.* .... R – R2; *20.* P – Kt6, Q × Q; *21.* P × R, Q × R; *22.* R × Q, Kt – Kt3; *23.* R – Kt1.

| 20. P × P | R – Kt4 |

Or *20.* .... Q × Q; *21.* R × Q, and Black has to give up a piece for the QRP.

21. Q—B7	Kt—Kt3
22. P—R7	B—R6
23. KR—Kt1	R × R ch
24. R × R	P—B4

If 24. .... Kt—Q4; 25. Q—Kt8, and White makes a fresh Queen.

25. B—B3	P—B5

Hoping for Q or R × Kt when P × P gives Black counter-chances, but White is remorselessly accurate.

26. P × P	resigns

Since if 26. .... R × P; 27. R × Kt, R × B; 28. P—R8=Q ch, R—B1; 29. Q × BP ch.

NIMZOVITCH

Shortly before the First World War a group of young players was coming to the fore (Nimzovitch, Réti, Breyer, and Tarta-kower) that was eventually to be known as the 'hyper-modern school'. These as writers and players revivified the game in practice and principle. All had great gifts for chess and were even more gifted in their writings. They were masters of daring paradox, the most extreme being Breyer's 'after 1. P—K4, White's game is in the last throes'. Still, as they themselves pointed out, they were not contradicting the main principles of modern chess but merely carrying on where Steinitz left off.

Perhaps the greatest of this school was Aron Nimzovitch, who was born in 1886 in Riga (then Russia), but spent the latter half of his short life in Denmark. He adopted Danish nation-ality and died in Copenhagen in 1935. If his tournament career was not so rich in successes as Lasker's or Capablanca's, he still had some great achievements to his credit, such as first prize at Copenhagen 1923, Dresden 1926, Hannover 1926, and above all Carlsbad 1929 (ahead of Capablanca).

In his play he produced some of the most extraordinary com-binations on record; but the seemingly mysterious art with which he contrived to bewitch and ensnare his opponents was based not so much on his combinative genius as on a strict adherence to the system he so brilliantly described in his writings. Consider the following strange masterpiece, Dresden 1926:

English Opening

WHITE: A. NIMZOVITCH BLACK: A. RUBINSTEIN

1.	P—QB4	P—QB4
2.	Kt—KB3	Kt—KB3
3.	Kt—B3	P—Q4
4.	P×P	Kt×P
5.	P—K4	

The first paradox; he gives himself a backward Pawn in order to gain rapid development and a fine field of action for his KB.

5.	....	Kt—Kt5

Not so strong as it loooks; better is 5. .... Kt×Kt; 6. KtP× Kt, P—KKt3.

6.	B—B4	P—K3

Bad for Black is 6. .... Kt—Q6 ch; 7. K—K2, Kt×B ch; 8. R×Kt, when White has a great advantage in development.

7.	O—O	QKt—B3

Instead of this, which leaves Black's other Knight exposed to attack, Nimzovitch advises 7. .... P—QR3.

8.	P—Q3	Kt—Q5
9.	Kt×Kt	P×Kt
10.	Kt—K2	

Threatening 11. B—Kt5 ch, and if B—Q2; 12. Kt×P, hence Black's next move.

10.	....	P—QR3
11.	Kt—Kt3	B—Q3
12.	P—B4	O—O
13.	Q—B3	K—R1

A good plan. Black wants to stop the advance of White's KBP

by P—B4, but cannot do so until his King is off the diagonal of White's KB.

14. B—Q2	P—B4
15. QR—K1	Kt—B3
16. R—K2	Q—B2

This natural-looking move is a mistake. Instead he should play *16. .... B—Q2; 17. P×P, P×P; 18. KR—K1, Q—B3;* (this is why Q—B2 was wrong) and Black should hold the game.

| 17. P×P | P×P |

Black (Rubinstein)

White (Nimzovitch) to play

The problem now arises – how should White continue his attack on the K side? Nimzovitch's solution has a most original savour.

18. Kt—R1

Aiming at KKt5.

18.	B—Q2
19. Kt—B2	QR—K1
20. KR—K1	R×R
21. R×R	Kt—Q1

If *21. .... R—K1; 22. Q—Q5.*

| 22. Kt—R3 | B—B3 |

R—K1 again fails; this time against *23*. Q—R5, R×R; *24*. Kt—Kt5, P—R3; *25*. Q—Kt6, P×Kt; *26*. Q—R5 mate.

23. Q—R5	P—KKt3
24. Q—R4	K—Kt2
25. Q—B2	

Another mysterious but logical manoeuvre. As will be seen, the Queen moves to and fro solely in order to divert one of Black's defensive pieces from the K side.

25.	B—B4
26. P—QKt4	B—Kt3
27. Q—R4	R—K1
28. R—K5	Kt—B2

If *28*. .... R×R; *29*. P×R, Q×P; *30*. Q—R6 ch, K—B3; *31*. Q—B8 ch, Kt—B2; *32*. Q×Kt mate.

29. B×Kt	Q×B

Or *29*. .... R×R; *30*. P×R, Q×B; *31*. Kt—Kt5, Q—Kt1; *32*. P—K6, B—Q4; *33*. Q—B4, followed by Q—K5 ch and wins.

30. Kt—Kt5	Q—Kt1
31. R×R	B×R
32. Q—K1	B—B3

If *32*. .... K—B1; *33*. Q—K5, B—Q1; *34*. Kt—K6 ch, K—K2; *35*. Q—B5 ch, K—Q2; *36*. Kt—B8 ch, winning the Queen.

33. Q—K7 ch	K—R1

He is mated or loses the Queen after *33*. .... K—R3; *34*. Kt—K6.

34. P—Kt5!	

Bringing the Bishop into final powerful action.

34.	Q—Kt2

Giving up a piece which is equivalent to resignation. But if *34*. .... P×P; *35*. Kt—K6, P—R4; *36*. Q—B6 ch, K—R2;

37. Kt−Kt5 ch, K−R3; *38.* B−Kt4, followed by B−B8 ch.

White finished off the game with *35.* Q × Q ch, K × Q; *36.* P × B, P × P; *37.* Kt−B3, P−B4; *38.* Kt−K5, B−B2; *39.* Kt−B4, K−B2; *40.* P−Kt3, B−Q1; *41.* B−R5, B−K2; *42.* B−B7, K−K3; *43.* Kt−Kt6, P−R3; *44.* P−KR4, P−Kt4; *45.* P−R5, P−Kt5; *46.* B−K5, resigns.

ALEKHINE

Capablanca's reign as world champion was brief – from 1921 to 1927, when he was defeated, unexpectedly, by the Franco-Russian Alekhine.

Alexander Alekhine was born in Moscow in 1892. He left Russia after the Revolution and went to live in Paris where he acquired French citizenship. During the Second World War he left France for Portugal and he died there at Estoril in 1946.

He had a vast tournament record, taking part as he did in many more events than either Lasker or Capablanca. The really outstanding successes commence after the First World War. In 1921 he won three first prizes – at Triberg, The Hague, and Budapest. He was first again at Baden Baden 1925, Kecskemet 1927, San Remo 1930, Bled 1931, Berne and London 1932, Zurich 1934, Dresden 1936, and at many other smaller tournaments. In matches he beat Bogoljubow twice, Euwe twice (and lost to him once), and won the great match against Capablanca at Buenos Aires in 1927 by +6, −3, =25.

Alekhine was the most versatile of all chess geniuses, being equally at home in every style of play and in all phases of the game. Added to this universal quality was an apparently inexhaustible power of producing miraculously beautiful combinations so that he has left us a heritage of more fine games than any other chess master.

In 1938 I was playing in the same tournament as Alekhine at Margate, and still vivid in my memory is the following game which is typical of his imaginative genius. It was played in Round Six, and though I myself was engaged in winning a game by a sacrificial K-side attack against the woman world champion,

Miss Menchik, I can well remember how passionately absorbed I and everyone else was in Alekhine's great combination. Margate 1938:

Queen's Gambit Accepted

WHITE: A. ALEKHINE		BLACK: E. E. BÖÖK	
1. P—Q4	P—Q4	4. P—K3	P—K3
2. P—QB4	P×P	5. B×P	P—B4
3. Kt—KB3	Kt—KB3	6. O—O	Kt—B3

More exact is P—QR3 at once.

7. Q—K2	P—QR3
8. Kt—B3	P—QKt4

Black leaves his King too long in the centre. He should play B—K2 and get castled as soon as possible.

9. B—Kt3	P—Kt5

If 9. .... B—K2; White gains a strong initiative by 10. P×P, B×P; 11. P—K4, followed by P—K5. From now on White conducts the attack with wonderful verve.

10. P—Q5!	Kt—QR4

10. .... P×Kt; 11. P×Kt; P×P; 12. B×KtP, opens up the position in White's favour since his two raking Bishops are immensely powerful.

11. B—R4 ch	B—Q2
12. P×P	P×P
13. R—Q1!	

White has conceived a beautiful combination based on the presence of the Black King in the centre – the Rook, as well as the Knight, is to be sacrificed.

13.	P×Kt
14. R×B!	Kt×R
15. Kt—K5	R—R2
16. P×P!	

Much better than *16*. Q — R5 ch, P — Kt3; *17*. Kt × P, P × Kt; *18*. Q × R, K — B2; which is in favour of Black.

Black (Böök) to play

223

White (Alekhine)

16. ....   K — K2

Böök, a truly sporting player who was as much taken with this game as the spectators, subsequently annotated it in the *British Chess Magazine* and pointed out there that after *16*. .... P — Kt3 White could continue the attack by *17*. Q — Q3, K — K2; *18*. P — K4, Kt — KB3; *19*. Q — B3, B — Kt2; *20*. B — KKt5, and now (*a*) *20*. .... R — B1; *21*. R — Q1, Q — B2; *22*. Kt — Q7, Q × Kt; *23*. R × Q ch, R × R; *24*. B × R, K × B; *25*. Q — Q3 ch, K — B1; *26*. Q × P ch, Kt — Kt2; *27*. Q — B6 ch, K — Kt1; *28*. B — B4 ch, K — R2; *29*. B — B7, followed by mate.

Or (*b*) *20*. .... Q — Kt3; *21*. Kt — Q7, R × Kt; *22*. P — K5, R — KB1; *23*. B × R, P — R3; *24*. P × Kt ch, B × P; *25*. B × RP, B — Kt2; *26*. Q — K3, B × B; *27*. Q × B, Q — Kt7; *28*. R — KB1, Q × RP; *29*. Q — Kt7 ch, R — B2; *30*. Q × P, R — B1; *31*. Q — Kt5 ch, K × B; *32*. Q × P, K — K1; *33*. R — Q1, and wins.

17.	P — K4	Kt — KB3
18.	B — KKt5	Q — B2
19.	B — B4	Q — Kt3

Or *19*. .... Q — Kt2; *20*. Q — K3, K — Q1; *21*. Q — Q3 ch

K — B1 ; *22.* R — Kt1, Q × P ; *23.* Kt — B7 !, Q × Q ; *24.* R — Kt8 mate.

    20. R — Q1

Threatening B — KKt5 followed by Q — R5.

20.	P — Kt3
21. B — KKt5	B — Kt2
22. Kt — Q7	R × Kt
23. R × R ch	K — B1
24. B × Kt	B × B
25. P — K5	resigns.

For if *25.* .... B — K2 ; *26.* Q — B3 ch, leads to mate in a few moves.

BOTVINNIK

The world champion, Mikhail Botvinnik, was born in St Petersburg in 1911. After qualifying to be an electrical engineer in the Leningrad Polytechnic he left Leningrad for Moscow where he now resides.

Botvinnik has won the Soviet championship seven times so far ; in 1931, 1933, 1939, 1941, 1944, 1945, and 1952. His other principal tournament successes are : equal first at Moscow 1935, and Nottingham 1936, first at Groningen 1946, Moscow 1947, and the world championship tournament 1948. His match record is more uneven. He drew with Flohr in 1933 and Levenfish in 1937, but won easily against Ragosin in 1940. He has also played six world championship matches : drew with Bronstein 1951, with Smyslov 1954, lost to Smyslov 1957, regained his title 1958, lost to Tal 1960, and beat him in 1961.

His play is distinguished by particularly deep strategy. Though his opening repertoire is limited, as was Capablanca's, yet he is the acknowledged authority on those openings that he does play and he has contributed much to standard theory in the Queen's Pawn openings and in the French Defence. In addition some of the best endings of recent years are to be found in his games.

The depth in his strategy is shown in the following game from the 1948 world championship tournament.

Queen's Gambit Declined, Half Slav Defence

WHITE: M. BOTVINNIK   BLACK: M. EUWE

	WHITE	BLACK
1.	P—Q4	P—Q4
2.	P—QB4	P—K3
3.	Kt—KB3	Kt—KB3
4.	Kt—B3	P—B3
5.	P—K3	QKt—Q2
6.	B—Q3	B—Kt5

This pin does not achieve much; better is 6. .... B—Q3.

| 7. | P—QR3 | B—R4 |
| 8. | Q—B2 | Q—K2 |

And here Black would do better to castle and if 9. O—O, B—B2; 10. P—K4, P×BP; 11. B×P, P—K4;

| 9. | B—Q2 | P×P |

Castles was still to be preferred.

| 10. | B×BP | P—K4 |
| 11. | O—O | O—O |

Not 11. .... P—K5; 12. Kt×P.

| 12. | QR—K1 | |

A far-sighted move. Botvinnik sees that Black will eventually play P—K5 and therefore prepares to support the KP so as to be able to reply with P—KB3. The KR is wanted on KB1 where it can profit from the opening of that file.

| 12. | .... | B—B2 |
| 13. | Kt—K4 | |

Threatening B—Kt4.

| 13. | .... | Kt×Kt |
| 14. | Q×Kt | P—QR4 |

Better is 14. .... Kt—B3; 15. Q—R4, P—K5; 16. B—Kt4, B—Q3; 17. B×B, Q×B; 18. Kt—Kt5, B—B4; 19. P—B3, QR—K1; and Black has good chances of holding the game.

15. B—R2	Kt—B3
16. Q—R4	P—K5
17. Kt—K5	B×Kt
18. P×B	Q×KP
19. B—B3	

White's Pawn sacrifice has given him two strong Bishops and possibilities of a K-side attack.

19.	Q—K2

Not *19.* .... Q—R4; *20.* B×Kt.

20. P—B3	

Reaching the position Botvinnik had envisaged when making his 12th move.

20.	Kt—Q4

Black (Euwe)

224

White (Botvinnik) to play

The exchange of Queens in no way diminishes White's attack, but other lines are still worse, e.g. (*a*) 20. .... B—K3; *21.* P×P!, B×B; *22.* R×Kt, B—K3; *23.* R—Kt6!, Q×Q; *24.* R×P ch, K—R1; *25.* R×BP dis ch, K—Kt1; *26.* R—Kt7 ch, K—R1; *27.* R—Kt5 dis ch, followed by mate, or (*b*) 20. .... P×P; *21.* B—Kt1, P—R3; *22.* R×P, Kt—Q4; *23.* R—Kt3, Q×Q; *24.* R×P ch, K—R1; *25.* R—R7 db ch, K—Kt1; *26.* R—R8 mate.

21. Q×Q	Kt×Q
22. P×P	P−QKt3
23. R−Q1	

Threatening 24. R×P, R×R; 25. R−Q8 mate.

23.	Kt−Kt3
24. R−Q6	B−R3
25. R−B2	B−Kt4
26. P−K5	

And now he threatens 27. P−K6, P×P; 28. R−Q7.

| 26. .... | Kt−K2 |

Hoping for time to play Kt−Q4 and so check the force of White's Bishops.

| 27. P−K4 | P−B4 |
| 28. P−K6 | P−B3 |

If 28. .... P×P; 29. R×KP, R×R; 30. K×R, K−B1; 31. R×P, with an easy win for White.

29. R×KtP	B−B3
30. R×B	Kt×R
31. P−K7 dis ch	R−B2
32. B−Q5	resigns

as he loses a piece after 32. .... R−QB1; 33. P−K8=Q ch, R×Q; 34. B×Kt, R−QB1; 35. B−Q5.

*   *   *

This brief review of the great players who have made chess history and theory has perforce omitted many important figures: Staunton, prime mover in the first international tournament at London in 1851; Zukertort, Steinitz's rival for many years; Tchigorin, the originator of some of the main variations in modern openings; Pillsbury, winner of the great international tournament at Hastings 1895; Maroczy and Schlechter, two great tournament players of the early twentieth century; Rubinstein, probably the strongest player never to have won the world championship; Spielmann, master of the brilliant attack; two of the chief members of the hyper-modern school, Réti and Tarta-kower, both of whom have produced a wealth of beautiful games; and the many great players who adorn the present-day chess arena. Euwe, Petrosian, Keres, Smyslov, Bronstein, Boleslavsky, Fine, Reshevsky, Najdorf, Szabo, Stahlberg, Geller, etc.

However, the reader will have obtained a glimpse of the evolution in style from the early nineteenth century to the present time. Further information can be obtained by reading the books in the list of recommended literature in the Bibliography.

CHAPTER 10

TOURNAMENT CHESS

THE spirit in which tournament games are played is, or should be, much different from the normal club game or friendly encounter. The atmosphere is more tense and, when so much depends on the extra point or half point, the rivalry is keener and more stern.

When the tournament is an important international event this tension is even more accentuated. Not only are the players themselves wrought up, as it were, into an ecstasy of concentration, but the numerous spectators thronging round a vital game share in and contribute to the excitement. For it must not be thought that chess events are without their spectacular appeal. I have seen large halls packed with people gazing with rapt attention at games in progress on the stage. In Mosców queues of enthusiasts, unable to gain entrance to the national championship, will wait patiently outside to hear the moves and results. Once when I was playing in the first round of a great international tournament at Bucharest, 1953, I emerged from deep thought to become conscious of a dull but persistent hammering that seemed to come from outside the building. After a time it stopped and I subsequently learnt that the noise had been due to a crowd of disappointed would-be spectators who, unable to gain admittance to an already full hall, beat at the gates in an attempt to force their way in and dispersed only when the police were fetched.

This is a somewhat extreme case, but all the same a crowd of onlookers, however quiet, causes an undercurrent of expectancy that often influences the game just as much as the situation of the players in the tournament table. Let me transport the reader for a brief while in his imagination to one of the exciting scenes of an international tournament. The event is the annual Hastings Chess Congress lasting from 30 December 1953 to 9 January 1954. It is the seventh round and David Bronstein, a grandmaster of the U.S.S.R., is leading in the Premier Tournament with 4½ points out of 6, just ½ point ahead of the British international master, C. H. O'D. Alexander. Now these two are due to meet and everything hangs on the result of their game. A draw will mean that Bronstein retains his lead with a very good chance of keeping it for the rest of the tournament. A loss for Alexander will make Bronstein's final victory in the tournament a practical certainty. Only a win for the home player can change the course of events in his favour, and, as he has Black, all experts agree that this result is most unlikely.

Many games in ten different sections are in progress but the players in the Premier Tournament are in a separate division at one end of the hall and are roped off from the crowd of spectators that has come in especially to view the Bronstein–Alexander encounter. This turns out to be something well worth watching. Bronstein takes the opening too lightly and is soon in difficulties. He offers a draw but Alexander, now a good Pawn up, rightly refuses and even goes on to win a second Pawn. The Russian grandmaster fights desperately hard to avoid defeat and lavishes all his ingenuity on the position. All in vain however against Alexander's great play which is a just blend of combinative skill and meticulous accuracy. The result means that Alexander leads instead of Bronstein; but as he drops a half point in the next round and both leaders win in the ninth and last round, first prize in this, the most interesting Hastings International Tournament for many years, is shared by Alexander and Bronstein.

The game that follows should not deter the reader by its length. It is a fascinating example of modern chess, and though, as a rule, few games go to more than about 50 or 60 moves, a total of 120 moves is far from being a record.

Queen's Pawn, Dutch Defence

WHITE: D. BRONSTEIN   BLACK: C. H. O'D. ALEXANDER

   1. P—Q4   P—KB4

   2. P—K4

A gallant decision; instead of playing the safe *2.* P—QB4, P—K3; *3.* P—KKt3, he opens up the game with the lively Staunton Gambit.

2.	P × P
3. Kt—QB3	Kt—KB3
4. P—B3	

Making certain that Black accepts the gambit Pawn. He can also play *4.* B—KKt5, Kt—B3; *5.* P—Q5, Kt—K4; *6.* Q—Q4 Kt—B2; with equal chances.

4.	P × P
5. Kt × P	P—KKt3

He refrains from playing *5.* .... P—Q4; because of *6.* Kt—K5, and if *6.* .... B—B4; *7.* P—KKt4, followed by P—Kt5 when White has a strong attack; but the text move also has its dangers.

6. B—KB4	B—Kt2
7. Q—Q2	

This serves the dual purpose of preparing to Castle Q and at the same time threatening to exchange off his QB for Black's KB when Black's K side will be weak.

7.	O—O
8. B—KR6	P—Q4
9. B × B	K × B
10. O—O—O	

Not the best way of retaining the initiative since it allows Black to develop his QB usefully.

Correct is *10.* B—Q3, when Black cannot play *10.* .... B—B4; because of *11.* B × B, P × B; *12.* Q—Kt5 ch, with great advantage to White.

10.	B—B4!
11. B—Q3	B × B
12. Q × B	Kt—B3

The exchange of Bishops has greatly helped Black. The one

remaining weakness in his position is on the K file where the KP is backward and White has a hold on Black's K4. He therefore sets to work to eliminate this by getting his KP advanced to K4.

13. QR–K1	Q–Q3
14. K–Kt1	P–QR3

Preventing White's Kt–QKt5 which would not have been effective the move before owing to 14. Kt–QKt5, Q–B5 ch.

15. R–K2	QR–K1
16. KR–K1	P–K3
17. Kt–K5	

Not a good move since he cannot maintain the Kt in its advanced position and must soon waste time in retreat. It would be better to give the King an outlet by P–QR3 and then to play for a K-side attack by P–R3 and P–KKt4.

17.	Kt–Q2
18. Kt–B3	R–B4
19. R–K3	

Black (Alexander) to play

225

White (Bronstein)

19.	P–K4

The advance has been achieved; Black's last weakness has disappeared and he enjoys the initiative in addition to his extra Pawn.

20. P × P	Kt(Q2) × P	23. R × R	Q × R
21. Kt × Kt	R(B4) × Kt	24. Q × QP	Q × P
22. R × R	R × R	25. Q – Q7 ch	

Not a good check since it leaves the KtP unprotected. Again he would be better advised to give his King a flight square by P – R3.

25.	K – R3
26. P – R3	Q – Q3

It is better to keep the Queen in the centre like this rather than to take the pawn by 26. .... Q × P; when 27. Q × P, makes it impossible for Black to protect his other Q-side pawns.

27. Q – B8	Kt – Q1
28. P – KKt4?	

The advance of the KKtP renders it more and more liable to attack. He should play 28. Q – R3 ch.

28.	K – Kt2
29. P – Kt3	P – B3
30. P – Kt5	

This further weakens the Pawn; better is 30. K – Kt2.

30.	Q – K2!

A strong move that by means of the twofold attack on White's Pawns forces the eventual win of a second Pawn.

31. Q – Kt4	Kt – B2	34. Kt – Q6	Kt × Kt
32. Kt – K4	Q × RP	35. Q – B6 ch	K – Kt1
33. Q – K6	Q – R4	36. Q × Kt	

White has no more useful checks since 36. Q – K6 ch, is met by 36. .... Kt – B2. We now have a Queen-and-Pawn ending that demands great patience and skill on Black's part since, though he is two Pawns up, his King is vulnerable to checks and he always has to beware of the possibility of a draw by perpetual check.

Black must achieve two aims. The more immediate is to make his King safe from check; whilst the eventual winning manoeuvre is to create a passed Pawn on the K side.

Black (Alexander) to play

226

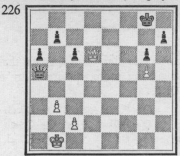

White (Bronstein)

36.	Q – K8 ch	41. P – Kt4	Q – K5
37. K – R2	Q – K1	42. Q – Q8 ch	K – B2
38. Q – B7	P – Kt4	43. Q – B6 ch	K – K1
39. K – Kt1	Q – K8 ch	44. Q – Q6	
40. K – Kt2	Q – K3		

Or 44. Q – R8 ch, K – Q2; 45. Q × P ch, K – Q3; 46. P – B3, Q – Kt7 ch; 47. K – Kt3, Q × P; and already Black has achieved the above-mentioned objective of creating a passed Pawn on the K side.

44.	Q – Q4	48. Q – Kt7 ch	Q – Q2
45. Q – B6	K – Q2	49. Q – K5 ch	Q – Q3
46. Q – Kt7 ch	K – Q3	50. Q – Kt7 ch	K – Kt3
47. Q – B6 ch	K – B2	51. Q – B3	

Capture of the KRP would be still worse now because of 51. Q × RP, Q × P ch; 52. K – R2, Q – K5; 53. K – Kt1, P – R4; and White cannot prevent the eventual advance of this Pawn to R6 with mating threats, whilst his KKtP is still liable to attack.

51.	Q – K2	55. Q – Q4 ch	K – Kt2
52. Q – Q4 ch	K – Kt2	56. Q – R8	Q – Q2
53. P – B3	Q – QB2	57. K – R3	Q – K2
54. Q – R8	K – Kt3	58. Q – B6	Q – QB2

A terrible mistake would be *58. .... Q×Q; 59. P×Q,* when the Black King cannot reach the KBP in time to stop it queening.

    59. K – Kt2   P – QR4

So as to give his own King more space and at the same time to render the opposing King more vulnerable by removing the protection of the QKtP.

60. P×P	Q×P	*63.* Q – Q7 ch	K – Kt3
61. Q – K6	Q – B2	*64.* Q – Q8 ch	K – B4
62. K – Kt3	Q – B5	*65.* Q – K7 ch	K – Kt3

A momentary vacillation after which he again pursues the correct plan of bringing his King over to the K side to attack White's KKtP.

66. Q – Q8 ch	K – B4	*69.* Q – Kt4	Q – B4
67. Q – K7 ch	K – Q4	*70.* Q – Q7 ch	K – K4
68. Q – Q7 ch	Q – Q3	*71.* Q×RP	

He might as well take the RP since Black is now ready to enforce his attack on the KKtP by K – B5.

    71. ....   K – B4

Black (Alexander)

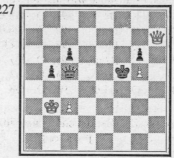

227

White (Bronstein) to play

    72. Q – Q7 ch

If 72. Q−R6, Q−Q4 ch; 73. K−R3, Q−Kt7 and the KKt
Pawn falls, and similarly if 72. Q−R4, Q−Q4 ch; followed by
Q−Kt7 wins.

72.	K × P
73. Q−Q2 ch	K−B3
74. Q−Q8 ch	K−B2
75. Q−B7 ch	Q−K2
76. Q−B4 ch	

If 76. Q × P, Q−K3 ch; exchanging Queens with a won Pawn
ending.

76.	K−Kt2
77. Q−Q4 ch	Q−B3
78. Q−K4	K−B2
79. K−Kt2	

Black was threatening Q−K3 ch.

79.	Q−Q3
80. Q−B3 ch	Q−B3
81. Q−K4	P−Kt4
82. Q−R7 ch	K−K3
83. Q−K4 ch	K−Q3

Black now intends to bring his King into safety on the Q side
before making a further advance with his KKtP.

84. Q−Q3 ch	K−B2	91. Q−K3 ch	Q−B4
85. Q−R7 ch	K−Kt3	92. Q−K8	Q−B7 ch
86. K−B2	Q−B5	93. K−Kt3	Q−B3
87. Q−K7	Q−B7 ch	94. Q−Q7	K−B4
88. K−Kt3	Q−Q7	95. K−B2	Q−K4
89. Q−K8	Q−Q4 ch	96. Q−Q8	Q−K5 ch
90. K−Kt2	Q−Q3		

Forcing forward the KKtP – the end is now in sight.

97. K−Kt2	P−KKt5
98. Q−Q7	

After 98. Q−B8 ch, K−B5; 99. Q−Kt4 ch, K−Q4; White
has no more checks.

98.	K — B5
99. Q — Q1	Q — Kt7 ch
100. K — R1	P — B4

The simplest and quickest way to win was by *100.* .... K × P; the move played also wins, but White's neat resource in reply had been overlooked by Black – understandably now fatigued through the long fight – and in consequence the game is a little prolonged.

Black (Alexander)

228

White (Bronstein) to play

101. Q — B2	Q — B8 ch

Not *101.* .... Q × Q; stalemate!

102. K — Kt2	K — Q4

With his last move White was even threatening to give mate by Q — K4.

103. Q — Q2 ch	K — K5

With the Pawns so far advanced, and with White's King also vulnerable, the Black King can venture right into White's territory; part of his defence is that he can eventually fend off a check with his Queen, in turn pinning the opposing Queen on the King.

104. Q—Kt5	Q—B4		
105. Q—R4	K—B6		
106. Q—R1 ch	K—K7		
107. Q—Kt2 ch	K—K8		
108. P—B4			

If *108.* Q—Kt1 ch, Q—B8; and then if *109.* Q × KtP, Q—K7 ch; or if *109.* Q × BP, Q—B7 ch; in both cases exchanging Queens with a won Pawn ending. This little end-game combination has a neat and pleasing symmetry.

108.	P—Kt5
109. Q—Kt1 ch	K—K7

Not now *109.* .... Q—B8; *110.* Q × BP, Q—B7 ch; *111.* Q × Q ch, K × Q; *112.* P—B5, P—KKt6; *113.* P—B6, P—Kt7; *114.* P—B7, P—Kt8=Q; *115.* P—B8=Q and draws.

110. Q—Kt2 ch	K—K6
111. K—Kt3	

If *111.* Q—Kt3 ch, K—Q5; and White cannot give another check without allowing Black to pick up his remaining Pawn.

111.	Q—Q6 ch	*115.* Q—K3 ch	K—Kt7
112. K—R4	Q × P	*116.* Q—K5 ch	Q—B6
113. Q—Kt3 ch	K—Q7	*117.* Q—Kt5	P—KKt6
114. Q—B2 ch	K—B6	*118.* Q—Kt4	P—Kt7

Since *119.* Q × KKtP ch, is met by *119.* .... Q—B7 ch; exchanging Queens.

119. Q—Kt5	Q—B8
120. Q × BP	

A last attempt; if *120.* .... Q × Q; stalemate! But Black is alive to this danger and plays

120.	Q—B7 ch!

whereupon White resigns. A remarkable game of which British chess can be justly proud.

CHAPTER 11

THE YOUNGER SCHOOL

IT is one of the entrancing aspects of chess that it is constantly renewing itself with a fresh series of great players and in the last ten years there has emerged a younger school that has been particularly notable for producing games full of interesting and adventurous chess. The best of these players have known how to blend the ideas they have inherited from their great predecessors, such as Alekhine and Botvinnik, with their own innovations. Their styles are varied; for though they have one thing in common – youth – they still derive from many diverse strands of chess knowledge and influence.

Very broadly speaking, one can divide them into two groups: the deeply strategical and the more tactical, highly combinative type of player. To the first group belong the Leningrad grandmaster, Boris Spassky, the United States of America twenty-year old genius Bobby Fischer, the Icelandic Fridrik Olafsson, and our own champion Jonathan Penrose. In the second are to be found the ex-world champion Mikhail Tal of Latvia and the Danish grandmaster Bent Larsen. I must emphasize that this does not mean that the members of the first group are not most accomplished in the art of combination or that those of the second are not great strategists as well as tacticians. In order to be a really great player one must be capable of excelling in all fields. But it does mean that the one group tends to favour its speciality more than the other.

Young though these players are, they have already taken part in so many international events that they have produced a wealth of fine games and have won many tournaments between them. In the interests of space I must confine myself to dealing with one representative of the tactical type – Tal – and one of the strategic – Fischer.

TAL

Mikhail Tal was born in 1936 in Riga, which was also the native town of Nimzovitch. His first important success came in 1953 when he won the Latvian Championship. His progress after this was extremely rapid. Coming equal fifth in his first Soviet Championship in 1956 he astonished the chess world by winning the title the following year and thus becoming, at the age of twenty, the youngest player ever to win the Soviet Championship. In 1957 he was a highly successful member of the Soviet team in the European Team Championship at Vienna and it was there that I met him for the first time. Two things about him struck me: his amazing speed of thought and his enormous enthusiasm for the game. Not content with the official hours of play he would fill in the gaps by playing quick games with whomsoever was ready to face him and even came to me one day with the request that a lightning tournament should be organized despite the crowded schedule of rounds that had to be completed in the team championship itself.

Retaining the Soviet title in the following year, he was now on the road that led to the world championship. At Portoroz in 1958 he came first in the inter-zonal tournament and the next year, after winning a strong international tournament at Zurich, he gained the right to challenge Botvinnik for the title by coming first in the candidates' tournament in Yugoslavia. In 1960 he crowned his chess career by beating Botvinnik in a match for the world championship at Moscow by $12\frac{1}{2}$–$8\frac{1}{2}$. His tenure of the world title was not a long one as he lost the return match to Botvinnik the following year. He had been handicapped in this encounter through ill-health, having had an operation not long before and in the candidates' tournament of 1962 he again fell ill and had to withdraw three-quarters of the way through the tournament. Still, he seemed to have recovered when last I met him at the 1962 Golden Sands Olympiad and the question as to his future career remains an open one. Such is his genius for the game that the possibility of a return to the world championship throne cannot be excluded. He is already one of the acknowledged immortals of the game.

Tal is the most imaginatively combinative player of the present age. This is what makes his games so attractive to the onlooker and, since this imagination is united with a wonderful capacity for deep calculation, this is what makes him so formidable an opponent for the very best players in the world. Occasionally, for example against Keres, he may overreach himself; but as a general rule his combinative gifts are so great as to render him irresistible when he has the attack. The particular mark of a Tal combination resides in the sudden nature of its arrival. At one moment the game may seem peaceful and undisturbed, but at the very next instant there comes a sudden flurry of movement and, almost before his opponent knows what has happened, he is in the midst of a violent storm.

Here, from an international tournament at Bled in the autumn of 1961 in which Tal won first prize, is an example of the fierce attacking in which Tal delights.

Sicilian Defence

WHITE: M. TAL   BLACK: F. OLAFSSON

1. P—K4	P—QB4
2. Kt—KB3	Kt—QB3
3. P—Q4	P×P
4. Kt×P	P—K3
5. Kt—QB3	Q—B2
6. B—K3	P—QR3
7. P—QR3	

A useful little move that serves three purposes: it prevents the pin of the Knight by Black's B—Kt5; it protects White's K Bishop from eventual exchange (after it has been developed on Q3); and finally it blunts a possible Black counter-attack by P—QKt4 – 5.

7.	Kt – B3
8. P – B4	P – Q3
9. Q – B3	B – K2
10. B – Q3	O – O
11. O – O	B – Q2
12. QR – K1	P – QKt4

Now there seems little point in this advance and one would prefer *12. ....* QR – B1

13. Q – Kt3	K – R1
14. Kt × Kt	B × Kt
15. P – K5	Kt – Kt1
16. Q – R3	Kt – R3

After this the storm breaks and Black has no defence that is adequate; better was *16. ....* P – Kt3.

Black (Olafsson)

229

White (Tal) to play

17. P – B5	Kt × P
18. R × Kt	P × R
19. B × BP	P – Kt3

Still worse for Black would be *19. ....* P – R3; *20.* B × P!

20. B–Q4	K–Kt1
21. P–K6	B–Kt4

He must prevent Q–R6; if instead 21. .... P–B3; White has a mating attack by 22. B×KtP, P×B; 23. Q–R6, B–Q1; 24. P–K7, B×KP; 25. Q×P ch, K–R1; 26. R–K3, followed by R–R3 ch.

22. P×P ch	R×P;
23. B×P	R–Kt2
24. Q–K6 ch	K–R1
25. B–K8	P–R3
26. B×B	Q×B
27. Kt–K4	R–K1
28. Q–Kt6	R–K2
29. P–KR4	Q–Q4

This does at any rate prevent any threatened mate since now he in turn threatens to free himself by R–K4; but now White is able to liquidate the position, regain the exchange and emerge two Pawns to the good into an easily won ending.

30. B×R ch	R×B
31. Q×P	Q×Q
32. Kt×Q	B×P
33. R–K8 ch	R–Kt1

No better is 33. .... K–R2; on account of 34. Kt–B5.

34. Kt–B7 ch	K–Kt2
35. R×R ch	K×R
36. Kt×P ch	K–R2
37. Kt–B5	B–Kt4
38. P–QKt3	K–Kt3

And Black resigned after making his 38th move.

FISCHER

Robert Fischer, or Bobby Fischer as he is more commonly called, belongs to the category of boy prodigies in chess history which has already produced such famous names as Capablanca and Reshevsky. He has however a special distinction, even amongst such exalted stars; for, at the moment of writing (1962), he must be regarded as the strongest chess-player of twenty years of age in the history of the game.

He is outstanding both in achievement and in quality. Already he has won the U.S.A. Championship four times in succession and his international record is almost equally impressive. At the Leipzig International Team Tournament he scored 13 points out of 18, on top board. In the 1961 Bled Tournament which Tal won, as already mentioned, he was second with 13½ points, a point behind Tal but a point ahead of such great players as Gligoric, Keres, and Petrosian who tied for third place. He was unbeaten in this tournament and even more impressive was his performance in the inter-zonal at Stockholm the following year where he was again unbeaten and where he came first with 17½ points out of 22, no less than 2½ points ahead of the Soviet grandmasters Geller and Petrosian who shared second place.

In May and June of 1962 came the candidates' tournament at Curaçao. The event proved a little disappointing for Fischer, since he started badly, with three losses in his first five games, and though he pulled up well later on, his final score of 14 left him in fourth place, with Petrosian the winner with 17½ points and Geller and Keres equal second with 17. Still, such a result at such an age is impressive enough and leaves one with the conviction that he will win the world championship title, if not in the immediate then in the near future – always provided the next few years are utilized by the young American for further self-improvement.

These results are striking, but even more impressive is the quality of his play which is marked by a maturity of judgement and a depth of strategy unexcelled in present-day chess. All his best games are distinguished by a classical strategic line that reminds one very much of Capablanca, whom, incidentally, he admits to have studied. His combinations, if lacking in that dream-like, mysterious character that pervades those of Tal, are still of the utmost competence; but they are used (and rightly so) to round off his strategic aims and are not regarded as goals in themselves. He is an attacking player – but essentially a sound attacking player inclined neither to overreach or underreach himself. Take for example the following game for which he was awarded a brilliancy prize at the Stockholm Inter-zonal Tournament of 1962. Note how, though he is on the aggressive from the very start, he does not attack without massing his pieces together. Note too how in the later stages of the game he makes classic use of the advantage of a well-placed minor piece over an in-differently placed one.

Sicilian Defence

WHITE: R. FISCHER   BLACK: J. BOLBOCHAN

1.	P–K4	P–QB4
2.	Kt–KB3	P–Q3
3.	P–Q4	P × P
4.	Kt × P	Kt–KB3
5.	Kt–QB3	P–QR3
6.	P–KR3	Kt–B3
7.	P–KKt4	Kt × Kt

Hoping to stem the force of White's attack, partly by exchanges and partly by the ensuing Pawn advance; but this does not seem to be quite adequate and a better scheme of defence lies in 6. .... P–KKt3.

8.	Q × Kt	P–K4
9.	Q–Q3	B–K2
10.	P–Kt5	

More aggressive than *10*. B – Kt2, as was played in the game Gereben–Geller, Budapest 1952, when it was Black who gained the attack after *10.* .... B—K3; *11.* P—Kt3, O—O; *12.* B—Kt2, P—QKt4; *13.* O—O—O, P—Kt5.

10.	Kt—Q2
11. B—K3	Kt—B4

Taking off the KtP leads to a very bad game for Black after *11.* .... B×P; *12.* B×B, Q×B; *13.* Q×P, Q—K2; *14.* Q×Q ch, K×Q; *15.* Kt—Q5 ch.

12. Q—Q2	B—K3
13. O—O—O	O—O

A better plan of defence was *13.* .... Q—B2 with the idea of castling Queenside.

14. P—B3	R—B1
15. K—Kt1	Kt—Q2

The obvious counter-attacking move of Q—R4 fails here on account of *16.* Kt—Q5.

16. P—KR4	P—Kt4
17. B—R3	B×B

Kt—Kt3 at once would result in the loss of a pawn after *18.* B×Kt, Q×B; *19.* Kt—Q5, Q—Q1; *20.* Kt×B ch, Q×Kt; *21.* Q×P.

18. R×B	Kt—Kt3

As will soon become apparent, Black now suffers from the fact that his Bishop is much worse placed than White's Knight. Since Black's Knight is a most useful defensive piece it would have been wiser to have retained it and played here *18.* .... R—K1; *19.* Kt—Q5, B—B1.

19. B×Kt	Q×B
20. Kt—Q5	Q—Q1
21. P—KB4	P×P
22. Q×P	Q—Q2
23. Q—B5!	

A strong move to which Black cannot reply *23. .... Q×Q;* because of *24. Kt×B ch,* winning a piece.

23.	QR−Q1
24. R−R3	Q−R2
25. R−QB3	

Threatening to win a piece by R−B7; he could have won a pawn here by *25. Kt×B ch, Q×Kt; 26. R×P,* but this would have released the pressure to some extent and would certainly not have been so forceful as the text-move.

25.	P−Kt3
26. Q−Kt4	Q−Q2
27. Q−B3	Q−K3

The effect of the strongly placed Knight is not only to deprive Black of any counter-attack but also to prevent him from any reasonable means of freeing his position. If now, for instance, *27. .... R−B1; 28. Kt−Kt6.*

28. R−B7	QR−K1

Again, if *28. .... R−Q2; 29. Kt−B4.*

29. Kt−B4	Q−K4
30. R−Q5	Q−R1
31. P−R3	

A quiet little move that shows the mastery White exerts over the board. Black now has no good move.

31.	P−R3
32. P×P	Q×P
33. P−R5	B−Kt4
34. P×P!	P×P

Black is hopelessly placed after *34. .... B×Kt; 35. P×P ch, R×P; 36. R×R, K×R; 37. R−B5 ch.*

Black (Bolbochan)

230

White (Fischer) to play

35. Q – QKt3 !

The *coup de grâce*; if now 35. .... K – R1; to avoid the discovered check, then 36. R × B, Q × R; (the foresight of White's 31st move is now clear since Black would have had here Q – R8 ch followed by mate if it were not for the outlet for White's King) 37. Q – R3 ch, K – Kt1; 38. Q – R7 mate.

    35. ....   R × Kt
    36. R – K5 dis ch   K – B1
    37. R × R ch   resigns.

Because of 37. .... K × R; 38. Q – K6 ch, K – B1; 39. Q – B8 and mates next move.

*   *   *

A parting word or two on how to improve your strength as a player. The first essential is practice, and this practice should be with players better than yourself. So join a chess club and become a member of the British Chess Federation. The B.C.F. runs a series of competitions for all classes of players every year. Next, play through the games of the masters and try to work out for yourself the reasons for the moves. Finally, study the endings. This part of the game is the great weakness of all amateurs; but it is a weakness that can easily be remedied.

Do not be content to remain at the same dull level of play all your life. Chess is a game which, the better you play the more you enjoy; its possibilities are almost infinite and so are its pleasures.

APPENDICES

ALGEBRAIC NOTATION

THE descriptive notation (page 16) is only used in English- and Spanish-speaking countries. Everywhere else the algebraic notation is used, and indeed the algebraic has even infiltrated into Anglo-Saxon circles of recent years. Deservedly so, as it is both more logical and more succinct than the descriptive.

The last edition of the rules of the International Chess Federation describes this notation as follows:

The pieces, with the exceptions of the Pawns, are represented by their initial letters. The Pawns are not specially indicated.

The eight files (from left to right for White) are represented by the letters from a to h. The eight ranks are numbered from 1 to 8, counting from White's first rank. (So, in the initial positions the White pieces are on the ranks 1 and 2 and the Black pieces on ranks 7 and 8.)

Thus each square is invariably defined by the combination of a letter with a number. To the initial letter of the pieces (except the Pawn) there is added the square of departure and the square of arrival. In the shortened form of notation the square of departure is omitted.

Thus: Bc1 – f4 = the Bishop on the square c1 is played to the f4 square. In shortened notation Bf4. Or: e7 – e5 = the Pawn on the square e7 is played to e5. In shortened notation e5.

When two similar pieces can go to the same square, the shortened notation is completed in the following way: if, for example, two Knights are on g1 and d2, the move Ktg1 – f3 would be written in the shortened form Ktg – f3. If the Knights are on g1 and g5, the move Ktg1 – f3 would in the shortened form be Kt1 – f3.

THE FORSYTH NOTATION

This is a handy way of noting down a position without using a diagram. Starting with the top rank of the board the initial letters of the pieces are put down from left to right. The vacant squares are indicated by a figure giving their number and the end of each rank is indicated by a sloping stroke. The White pieces are represented by capitals and the Black by ordinary letters.

Thus 2 B 1 r 1 k KT/8/ is equivalent to the following: (looking at it from White's point of view and employing the descriptive notation) two vacant squares on QR8 and QKt8, White Bishop on QB8, one vacant square on Q8, Black Rook on K8, one vacant square on KB8, Black King on KKt8, White Knight on KR8, all squares from QR7 to KR7 vacant.

CHESS ORGANIZATIONS

The basic unit of chess organizations in this country is the chess club. Some thousands of these exist and nearly all are affiliated to the various counties to which they belong. Groups of these counties are joined together to form unions (such as the Southern Chess Union, Midland Chess Union, Northern Chess Union, etc.) and these in turn form part of, and are controlled by, the British Chess Federation. Players can be individual members of the B.C.F. or else can be affiliated to the B.C.F. through their county – or even do both. Every year the Federation runs a number of national competitions: the Counties Championship, a National Club Championship, Individual Championships for both men and women, and a number of tournaments of lesser strength at the B.C.F. Congresses which take place in a different Union each year. Below is a list of the British Champions 1904–68.

1904	W. E. Napier	1910	H. E. Atkins
1905	H. E. Atkins	1911	H. E. Atkins
1906	H. E. Atkins	1912	R. C. Griffith
1907	H. E. Atkins	1913	F. D. Yates
1908	H. E. Atkins	1914	F. D. Yates
1909	H. E. Atkins	1915–19	No contest

1920	R. H. V. Scott	1951	E. Klein
1921	F. D. Yates	1952	R. G. Wade
1922	No Contest	1953	D. A. Yanofsky
1923	Sir George Thomas	1954	J. W. Barden and
1924	H. E. Atkins		A. Phillips
1925	H. E. Atkins	1955	H. Golombek
1926	F. D. Yates	1956	C. H. O'D. Alexander
1927	No Contest	1957	Dr Fazekas
1928	F. D. Yates	1958	J. Penrose
1929	Sultan Khan	1959	J. Penrose
1930	No Contest	1960	J. Penrose
1931	F. D. Yates	1961	J. Penrose
1932	Sultan Khan	1962	J. Penrose
1933	Sultan Khan	1963	J. Penrose
1934	Sir George Thomas	1964	M. J. Haggarth
1935	W. Winter	1965	P. N. Lee
1936	W. Winter	1966	J. Penrose
1937	W. A. Fairhurst	1967	J. Penrose
1938	C. H. O'D. Alexander	1968	J. Penrose
1939–45	No Contest	1969	J. Penrose
1946	R. F. Combe	1970	R. G. Wade
1947	H. Golombek	1971	R. D. Keene
1948	R. J. Broadbent	1972	B. R. Eley
1949	H. Golombek	1973	W. R. Hartston
1950	R. J. Broadbent		

All the national chess federations of the world are affiliated to the *Fédération Internationale des Échecs* (the International Chess Federation) which is concerned with international chess relationships and world chess in general. Every year a congress is held at which delegates from each national federation discuss the F.I.D.E. business. Once every two years an international team tournament is held. Since the Second World War the F.I.D.E. has taken over the organization of the individual world championships as well. This is done by a four-yearly cycle. In the first year zonal tournaments are held throughout the world. In the next year an inter-zonal tournament is contested. This consists of about twenty-two players who have qualified from the zonal tournaments. In the third year a knock-out series of

Candidates' matches between the first six from the inter-zonal and the first two of the previous candidates' series takes place. The winner of this plays a match in the following year against the existing world champion for the title. Thus in 1951 Bronstein, having won the candidates' tournament, played a match against the world champion Botvinnik. As Botvinnik drew the match he retained his title.

The list of world champions and their years of tenure are as follows: Steinitz 1886–94, Lasker 1894–1921, Capablanca 1921–7, Alekhine 1927–35, Euwe 1935–7, Alekhine 1937–46, Botvinnik 1948–57, Smyslov 1957–8, Botvinnik 1958–60, Tal 1960–61, Botvinnik 1961–3, Petrosian 1963–9, Spassky 1969–72, Fischer 1972–.

The F.I.D.E. recognizes some 160 players as international chess masters amongst whom are the following seven British players: C. H. O'D. Alexander, W. A. Fairhurst, H. Golombek, W. R. Hartston, R. D. Keene, D. Levy, and J. Penrose; in addition, from the Commonwealth there are C. J. S. Purdy and L. Steiner (Australia), F. Anderson and D. A. Yanofsky (Canada), and R. G. Wade (New Zealand). A recent development is the recognition of women chess masters, a title held by Mrs R. M. Bruce, Mrs J. Hartston, Mrs E. Pritchard, Miss A. Sunnucks, and Miss E. Tranmer.

SOME EXTRACTS FROM THE RULES OF CHESS
(As laid down by the International Chess Federation)

Touched Piece

Provided that he first warns his opponent, the player whose turn it is to move can adjust one or more pieces on their squares. Apart from the above case, if the player whose turn it is to move touches one or more pieces, he must make his move by moving or taking the first piece touched which can be moved or taken.

The touching of a piece or pieces entails no obligation if a breach of this rule is not pointed out by the opponent before he touches a piece, or if none of the moves indicated above can be carried out in accordance with the rules.

Illegal Positions

If during the game it is ascertained that an illegal move has been made, then the position shall be set up again as it was immediately before the making of the illegal move. The game shall then continue in accordance with the rules given in the above paragraph as regards the move replacing the illegal move. If it proves impossible to set up the position again then the game must be annulled and a fresh game played.

If, in the course of a game, one or more pieces have been accidentally displaced and are not correctly replaced, the position must be set up as it was immediately before the mistake and the game continued. If it proves impossible to set up the position again then the game must be annulled and a fresh game played.

If, after an adjournment, the position is incorrectly put up, then the position as it was on adjournment must be set up again and the game continued.

If during the game it is ascertained that the initial position of the pieces was incorrect, then the game must be annulled and a fresh game played.

If during the game it is ascertained that the initial position of the chessboard was incorrect, then the position that has been reached must be transferred to a chessboard that has been correctly placed and the game continued.

Drawn Game

The game is drawn:

1. When the King of the player whose turn it is to move is not in check and such player cannot make a move. This is called 'Stalemate'.
2. By agreement between the two players.
3. At the request of one of the players when the same position appears three times, and each time the same player has had the move. The position is considered the same if pieces of the same kind and colour occupy the same squares.

This right of claiming the draw belongs to the player:

(a) who is in a position to play a move leading to such repetition of the position, if he declares his intention of making this move; or (*b*) who is about to reply to a move by which such repeated position has been produced.

If a player makes a move without having claimed a draw in the manner prescribed in (*a*) or (*b*) he then loses this right to claim a draw; this right is however restored to him if the same position appears again with the same player having the move.

4. When the player whose turn it is to move proves that at least fifty moves have been played by each side without a capture of a piece and without a Pawn move having been made.

BIBLIOGRAPHY

HERE is a list of books that the reader will find of help in increasing his chess strength and knowledge. It is confined to books in English and those that were in print at the time of writing.

General Treatises

   Capablanca, J. R. *Chess Fundamentals*
   Lasker, Edward. *Modern Chess Strategy*

Openings

   Barden, L. W. *A Guide to Chess Openings*
   Fine, R. *Ideas Behind the Chess Openings*
   Griffith, R. C., and Golombek, H. *Pocket Guide to the Openings*
   Korn, W. *Modern Chess Openings*
   Sokolsky, A. P. *The Modern Openings in Theory and Practice*
   Suetin, A. S. *Modern Chess Opening Theory*

Middle Game

   Euwe, M. *Judgement and Planning in Chess*
   Keres, P., and Kotov, A. *The Art of the Middle Game*
   Nimzovitch, A, *My System*
   Pachman, L. *Modern Chess Tactics*
   Vukovic, V. *The Art of Attack in Chess*

End Game

   Averbach, J. *Chess Endings, Essential Knowledge*
   Euwe, M., and Hooper, D. *A Guide to Chess Endings*
   Fine, R. *Basic Chess Endings*
   Hooper, D. A. *A Pocket Guide to the End-Games*

Game Anthologies

   Euwe, M. *The Development of Chess Style*
   Gligorich, S. *Selected Chess Masterpieces*
   Reti, R. *Masters of the Chessboard*

Individual Game Collections

Alekhine, Dr A. *My Best Games of Chess*, 1908–23

Alekhine, Dr A. *My Best Games of Chess*, 1924–37

Alexander, C. H. O'D. *Alekhine's Best Games of Chess*, 1938–45

Clarke, P. H. *Tal's Best Games of Chess*

Fischer, R. *My 60 Memorable Games*

Golombek, H. *Capablanca's Best Games of Chess*

Keres, P. *Grandmaster of Chess*, Three volumes, *Early Games, Middle Years, Later Years of Paul Keres*

Larsen, B. *Selected Games of Chess*

Smyslov, V. *My Best Games of Chess*, 1935–1957

Tournament and Match Books

Clarke, P. H. 24*th U.S.S.R. Championship*

Golombek, H. 4*th Candidates*

General Information and Magazine

B.C.F. Year Book, published by the British Chess Federation, containing addresses of chess clubs, secretaries, set of chess rules, etc.

British Chess Magazine, published monthly. General Editor, B. P. Reilly; Games Editor, P. H. Clarke; Problem Editor, J. M. Rice.

INDEX

Openings

Middle Game

Endings

Individual Games

INDEX

MORE ABOUT PENGUINS
AND PELICANS

Penguinews, which appears every month, contains details of all the new books issued by Penguins as they are published. From time to time it is supplemented by *Penguins in Print*, which is a complete list of almost 5,000 titles.

A specimen copy of *Penguinews* will be sent to you free on request. Please write to Dept EP, Penguin Books Ltd, Harmondsworth, Middlesex, for your copy.

In the U.S.A.: For a complete list of books available from Penguins in the United States write to Dept CS, Penguin Books, 625 Madison Avenue, New York, New York 10022, U.S.A.

In Canada: For a complete list of books available from Penguins in Canada write to Penguin Books Canada Ltd, 2801 John Street, Markham, Ontario L3R 1B4.

a Penguin Handbook

THE ART OF THE MIDDLE GAME

Paul Keres and Alexander Kotov

TRANSLATED BY H. GOLOMBEK

Many chess-players know a large variety of openings and understand well the pattern of end games – but what happens in the middle? The difficulty of understanding the principles of middle-game play is perhaps best illustrated by the dearth of good books on the middle game. They can be counted on the fingers of one hand.

Yet the middle game is a real challenge to the player. Here in the full orchestration of the game the player has the chance to use all his pieces to carry out his ideas. All players will be grateful to the grandmasters, Keres and Kotov, for their masterly analysis of attack and defence in the middle game, and to Mr Golombek for his translation and fully authoritative introduction.

Of particular importance and interest are Kotov's complete chapter on the attack on the king, Keres's very personal analysis of defence, and Kotov's demonstration of the importance of pawn structure: the good player must know which pawn positions favour which types of attack and defence. Here is an essential addition to the chess-player's library.

FISCHER v. SPASSKY

REYKJAVIK 1972

C. H. O'D. Alexander and Francis Wyndham

This is the story of the World Championship match which made 1972 a year of unprecedented publicity for chess. The first part of the book, written before the match, gives an insight into the world of international competitive chess and the history of the World Championship, and deals with the events which led to Reykjavik, and the backgrounds of the two Grandmasters themselves – their lives, records and their previous encounters.

The second part, written during the championship, gives all the games of this epic match, fully annotated for the average player as well as the expert, complete with a unique collection of photographs and specially commissioned drawings.